2007 MASTERS® ANNUAL

—III—

Augusta National Golf Club

John Wiley & Sons, Inc.

Augusta National would like to recognize the contributions of writer Dick Mudry and photographers Sam Greenwood, Rusty Jarrett, Hunter Martin, Barry Koenig, and Mike Ehrmann.

Published by John Wiley & Sons, Inc., Hoboken, New Jersey
Published simultaneously in Canada

Wiley Bicentennial Logo: Richard J. Pacifico

Design and composition by Navta Associates, Inc.

For general information about our other products and services, please contact our Customer Care Department within the United States at (800) 762-2974, outside the United States at (317) 572-3993 or fax (317) 572-4002.

Wiley also publishes its books in a variety of electronic formats. Some content that appears in print may not be available in electronic books. For more information about Wiley products, visit our web site at www.wiley.com.

ISBN 978-0-470-22332-1 (special edition)
ISBN 978-0-470-22331-4 (trade edition)

Printed in Mexico

10 9 8 7 6 5 4 3 2 1

CONTENTS

2007
MASTERS®
ANNUAL

—— III ——

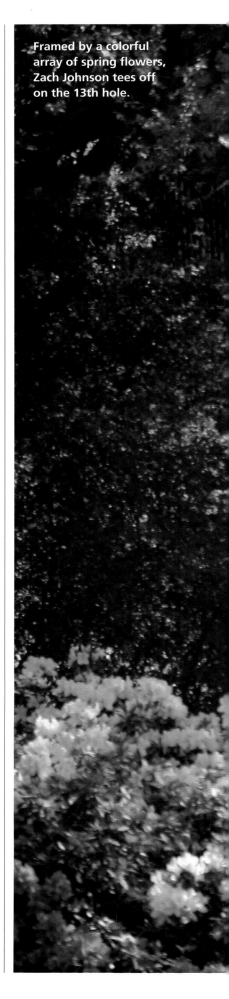

Framed by a colorful array of spring flowers, Zach Johnson tees off on the 13th hole.

Message from the Chairman

—— III ——

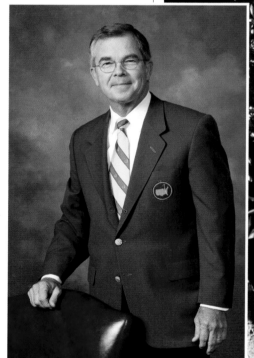

For many reasons, the 2007 Masters will be remembered as an historic event.

The winner, Zach Johnson, stuck to a carefully devised game plan and proved his mettle when it counted the most, on the final nine at Augusta National. Throughout the Tournament he battled gusty winds and brisk temperatures to defeat the greatest players in golf.

The record books will also note that the tradition of the Honorary Starter was back at the Masters. Thursday morning Arnold Palmer thrilled his army and returned to the first tee, where he rightly belongs. We were also able to celebrate Gary Player's 50th Masters. It was a truly remarkable feat for this three-time champion and our first international winner. The Masters Major Achievement Award, given to media members who covered the Masters 40 or more times, was also initiated. As was stated at the presentation, for decades the words of these 14 individuals defined our history. Now they are part of that history.

It was, however, a sad year with the loss of Byron Nelson. While Byron is no longer with us, this gentleman's accomplishments and spirit will live on as long as this Tournament is played.

I hope you enjoy this year's *Masters Annual*, and on behalf of Augusta National Golf Club I would like to thank everyone for a successful 2007 Masters. Next year's Tournament will be contested April 7 to 13.

Billy Payne

Magnolia Lane

Mickelson, Woods Building New Rivalry

— ||| —

Phil Mickelson and Tiger Woods appear on the verge of building a Masters rivalry like Sam Snead and Ben Hogan, and Arnold Palmer and Jack Nicklaus did in the past.

The Masters is built on tradition.

The tradition of providing the invitational field a tough but fair challenge over the 7,445-yard, par-72 Augusta National Golf Club course.

The tradition of the Green Jacket, a coat that signifies a special honor open only to the most proficient of players.

The tradition of honoring its champions. Cofounders Bobby Jones and Clifford Roberts willed it so.

And the tradition of rivalries, which are as common at the Masters as the blooming dogwoods and azaleas are across the former Fruitland Nurseries.

Rivalries have made individual events epic and their participants legends in the annals of golf.

From 1949 to 1954, Sam Snead and Ben Hogan combined to win five Masters titles. Jimmy Demaret, in 1950, was the only other player to manage a victory during this time.

From 1960 to 1966, Arnold Palmer and Jack Nicklaus won three Masters each, effectively shutting out the rest of the field

during that seven-year period except for Gary Player in 1961.

These days another rivalry is shaping up to equal or surpass the others.

You know the participants. One is a Tiger, as in Woods. The other is called Lefty, as in Phil Mickelson.

Woods and Mickelson have won five of the last six Masters titles heading into the 71st Tournament, with Canada's Mike Weir breaking the stranglehold in 2003.

Woods owns the 1997, 2001, 2002, and 2005 Masters titles. Mickelson was a winner in 2004 and 2006.

Like Snead and Hogan and Palmer and Nicklaus, they have also taken turns slipping the Green Jacket onto each other with great regularity.

That rivalry brought an added dimension to the 2007 Tournament.

And, said Palmer, the rivalry between Woods and Mickelson is good for the Masters and therefore good for the game of golf.

"I think it helps the game to have that kind of rivalry," said Palmer, a four-time

A smile was evident on Tiger Woods's face during a pre-Tournament moment.

Two-time champion Phil Mickelson was all business in defense of his 2006 Masters title.

Masters winner. "The more we can talk about Phil and his golf and the challenge to Tiger, I think that's good. I certainly have no problem with that being created."

Palmer will tell you that you need to recognize the fact that Woods and Mickelson are different people.

"They have different approaches," Palmer said of today's two stars. "Tiger has his approach and obviously it's quite good. And

Phil has his approach and it has been pretty successful, and just recently he started winning majors. If he continues, that's going to be the challenge to whomever he's playing against, whether it's Tiger or Charles Howell or some of the young guys that are just winning tournaments now. But I think the competition is what it's all about. I don't see Tiger backing off for a while."

Just as with Snead, Hogan, Palmer, and

Nicklaus, major tournaments such as the Masters remain the prime motivations for Woods and Mickelson. Major victories measure the two against the greats who came before them and provide a yardstick for those who will follow Woods at age 31, and Mickelson, 36, in this modern-day rivalry.

"It doesn't happen that often where we're both playing well at the same time, the same week, the same event," said Woods. "It's one of the hard dynamics of the game of golf. But we've definitely gone at it here in this event, [and] a couple of other events on the regular tour schedule. Any time you get to go at it with any of the top players in a major championship and they are playing well, it's always fun."

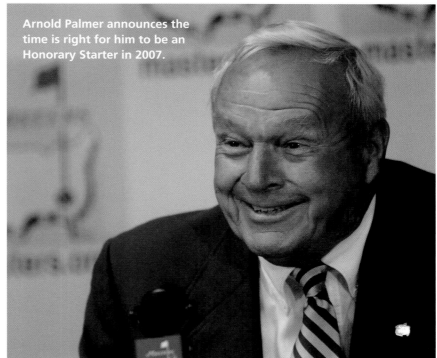
Arnold Palmer announces the time is right for him to be an Honorary Starter in 2007.

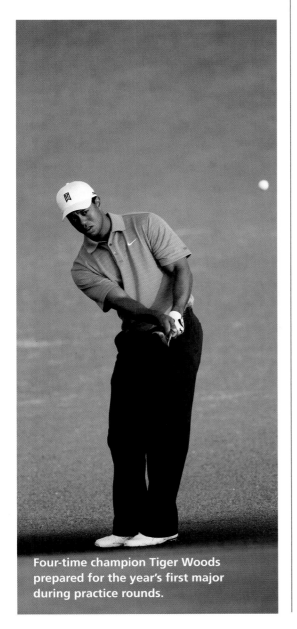
Four-time champion Tiger Woods prepared for the year's first major during practice rounds.

Masters History

5 years ago: Tiger Woods becomes only the third player to successfully capture consecutive Masters titles, joining Jack Nicklaus (1965–1966) and Nick Faldo (1989–1990) in that elite club.

10 years ago: At age 21, Tiger Woods becomes the youngest champion in Masters history, setting 20 records and tying six others, including the lowest 72-hole total and the widest margin of victory.

15 years ago: Fred Couples wins the Masters after his tee shot at No. 12 lands on the bank fronting the green but does not roll in the water. He makes par to win by two strokes over Raymond Floyd. Floyd sets the Tournament record for the oldest runner-up finisher (49).

20 years ago: Augusta native Larry Mize holes a 140-foot birdie chip from right of the green at No. 11 to defeat Greg Norman and Seve Ballesteros in a two-hole sudden-death playoff.

35 years ago: Jack Nicklaus wins his fourth Green Jacket and becomes the Tournament's third wire-to-wire winner, scoring 286 over 72 holes.

45 years ago: In the first Masters three-way playoff, Arnold Palmer defeats Gary Player and Dow Finsterwald by scoring 31 on the second nine. The 36-hole cut was changed to the low 44 plus ties.

55 years ago: Sam Snead defeats Jack Burke for his second Masters title. The first Masters Club dinner is held, hosted by Ben Hogan.

70 years ago: Byron Nelson wins his first Green Jacket by making up six strokes over two holes (Nos. 12 and 13) on the final day to defeat Ralph Guldahl by two strokes.

What They're Saying
(MONDAY–WEDNESDAY)

If you look at the past champions, there's a lot of foreign players that have won the Masters because in Europe they play in a lot of different adverse conditions and you have to be more creative when the conditions are tough, [and] then you have to have a better short game.

> —Mark O'Meara on how seven different international players—Sandy Lyle, Nick Faldo (three times), José Maria Olazabal (twice), Vijay Singh, Ian Woosnam, Mike Weir, and Bernhard Langer (twice)—have won 11 Green Jackets since 1988.

It's more difficult now. The golf course is playing certainly much longer, and you have to play the conditions as they are. I think it's fair and the condition is always great.

> —Two-time Masters winner Seve Ballesteros on seeing Augusta National's recent course changes for the first time in four years.

I'm heading into this week as prepared and as confident as I've ever been here.

> —Australian Adam Scott, a winner the week before the Masters, on his mind-set for the Tournament.

Surrounded by spring's vibrant colors, patrons enjoy the walk from the sixth tee to the green.

Mickelson opined on his prospects at the Masters as the 97-player field prepared for the 72-hole test once more.

Eight consecutive top-10 finishes heading into 2007 only bolstered Mickelson's confidence even more.

"I've played very well here in the past," Mickelson said. "It's certainly a course that I feel comfortable on and have played well here whether I've played well going in or not. I remember in '03 [that] I was playing terribly and was able to finish third. And when I've entered it playing well like last year, I've been able to win."

Woods said the reason the Masters has 16 multiple winners holding 44 titles in its 70-year history may be because familiarity does pay dividends.

"I think it's just understanding how to play it, where to miss it; shot selections," said Woods of the nuances of the Augusta National's course management.

"But once you figure it out, you see the same guys up there at the top of the board. Phil has been up there many times, and once he won a few years ago it gave him the confidence to do it again last year."

Both players came into Tournament week with victories in 2007.

Mickelson won the AT&T Pebble Beach National Pro-Am then lost a playoff to Charles Howell III at the Nissan Open the following week. Woods won the Buick Invitational and the WGC-CA Championship.

The two-time winner is relaxed, more so than ever before at the Masters.

"Do I look tense today?" Mickelson said Tuesday, a broad smile crossing his face.

Woods, meanwhile, was putting his game face on.

He had desperately wanted to win the 2006 Masters because his father, Earl, was very ill. Earl Woods passed away a month later, and Tiger's tie for third was painful.

With help from a range finder, former U.S. Open champion Jim Furyk checks the distance at the 14th hole.

Tiger Woods was looking for a fifth Masters title.

Gary Player, Arnold Palmer, and Jack Nicklaus enjoy Wednesday's relaxed Par 3 Contest atmosphere.

What They're Writing

(MONDAY–WEDNESDAY)

Shortly before 8:00 A.M. Thursday, one of the most recognizable swings in golf—a slashing, unstylish swing but one that wrote history will whip through the air over the first tee at Augusta National Golf Club, and the Masters will be under way.

Arnold Palmer is coming back to the scene of his four Masters victories, to the place where Arnie's Army was born, to the course where he ignited a surge in the popularity of golf with his charging style of play. But he won't need his full set of clubs. He's only going to hit one shot, a drive.

Arnie's the ceremonial starter of the Masters this week, carrying on one of the tournament's dearest traditions. It's a perfect fit.

—*Ron Green Sr.*, Charlotte Observer

A few zigzag turns from Augusta National Golf Club, at the end of a cul-de-sac on a leafy street, sits the house where Charles Howell III grew up.

When he was 7, his parents took him to the Masters tournament for the first time, and a local player named Larry Mize beat Greg Norman and Seve Ballesteros in a playoff. Howell's parents took him to the tournament the next year, and the next and the next. It all seemed so ordinary.

"I didn't have the appreciation for it as a kid that I do now," Howell said in a recent telephone interview. "It was just the hometown tournament. Little did I know."

—*Damon Hack*, New York Times

For some, it's that drive down Magnolia Lane. For others, it's eating a pimento cheese sandwich that comes wrapped in green wax paper. For others, it's a chance to walk the same soil trod by Bobby Jones, Ben Hogan and Arnold Palmer.

Each professional golfer has a different way of looking at their rookie experiences at the Masters.

"Just being in the clubhouse, sitting down and putting on my spikes in the locker room at Augusta," said Brett Quigley. "Does it get any better than that?"

—*Stan Awtrey*, Atlanta Journal-Constitution

Against a backdrop unlike anything else in sports—a tunnel of magnolia trees and walls of Georgia pines, vibrant azaleas, and the greenest grass you've ever seen—the 71st Masters is on our doorstep. For many, it's been that close for a while now.

"I think from a player's point of view," said defending champ Phil Mickelson, "we start thinking about it after the PGA [Championship] is finished [in August]. It's just fun to be part of the tournament, because history is made there every year."

—*Jim McCabe*, Boston Globe

The Masters Tournament is eternal.

What happens here this week seems as intrinsically tied with what happened 73 years ago as it will be 100 and 200 years from now.

That's the magic of this golf tournament and this place. It makes you feel like you're part of something forever.

That's what makes covering the Masters Tournament simultaneously one of the easiest and hardest things a journalist will ever do. Writers are always searching for the perfect word. But when it comes to describing one of the most hallowed events in sport, words can't do it justice.

—*Scott Michaux*, Augusta Chronicle

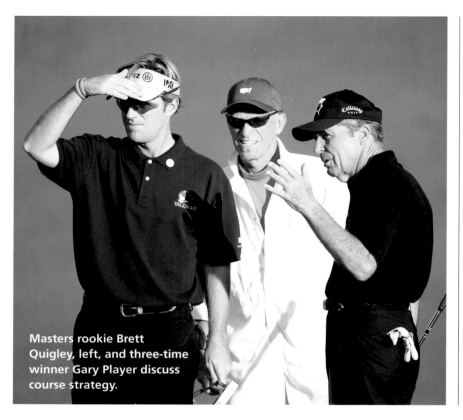

Masters rookie Brett Quigley, left, and three-time winner Gary Player discuss course strategy.

"Last year was a lot more difficult than I was letting on because I knew that was the last tournament he was ever going to watch me play," said Woods. "I just wanted to win one for his last time and didn't get it done, and it hurt quite a bit."

This Masters, Woods and his wife are expecting their first child in July.

Past champions recognize the skills that drive the latest Masters rivalry.

"I would say that certainly Tiger is always going to be at the top of anybody's list in any major championship or big event," said Mark O'Meara, the winner in 1998. "Phil has played well here, too, because he hits it far and has got a great short game."

A host of other professionals, such as past champion Vijay Singh, South African Ernie Els, England's Paul Casey, Australian Adam Scott, and Americans Charles Howell III, Chris DiMarco, and Chad Campbell may have a hand in the outcome.

U.S. Mid-Amateur champion Dave Womack, far left, plays a practice round with professionals Arron Oberholser, Phil Mickelson, and Chris DiMarco.

Gary Player

(MONDAY–WEDNESDAY)

He is likely one of the smallest Masters winners the Tournament has ever produced.

At 5-foot-7 and a fit-as-a-fiddle 150 pounds, Gary Player, age 71, looks up to many a man by the mere result of his diminutive size.

But along Augusta National Golf Club's fairways, the gregarious South African isn't shortchanged by his size in the least.

You can't win three Masters and be anything but a giant in heart.

"I've said that pound for pound he's the best golfer who ever lived," said six-time Masters winner Jack Nicklaus of Player. "He needed that competitiveness to compete. He didn't have the physical strength that some of the rest of us were blessed with, but he sure had the determination to win."

"I was pretty inspired when I read his autobiography," said U.S. Open champion Geoff Ogilvy, an Australian. "He proved you can come from a less-than-ideal scenario to the U.S. tour, and it was a long way from South Africa, especially 50 years ago. Very impressive." Multitime Masters winner Tiger Woods calls Player's accomplishments "truly remarkable," considering the global nature of his career.

"He was the first real global player," said Woods of Player. "I mean, he played everywhere."

Player came to the 71st Masters with his sights set on longevity, too.

He is playing his 50th Tournament, tying him with four-time winner Arnold Palmer for the most appearances in this annual rite of spring.

My how things have changed for Player since his 1957 debut.

These days jet travel to the Masters is relatively easy. But it wasn't always so.

His first trip took 40 hours of flying from Johannesburg, South Africa, to Augusta, with five stops along the way.

"It was [flying] in those Constellations . . . where you could hear [the engine] droning at 29,000 feet among the storms," he said. "I traveled with six children on those planes. I had to win the tournament to break even."

Player didn't win that Masters debut. He tied for 24th and earned $700. But he did become a masterful Masters winner.

Player won his first Green Jacket in 1961, becoming the first international player to do so. He added his second and third Masters titles in 1974 and 1978, respectively.

Twice he finished either second or tied for second, and once he finished third.

He has seen great changes in the Tournament over his half century of competition.

"The big difference between when I first played the Masters and now is that the ball travels 50 yards farther and there are grooves in clubs to help the ball go straight," said Player of how dramatically technology has changed golf in his career.

"The fairways are five times better and the bunkers have uniform sand because they have the machinery to keep it uniform. The biggest difference from when Arnold, Jack, and I played is the spike marks on the greens. There were hundreds then. Now there are none."

And his memories at the Masters are with him every day.

"I've had so many wonderful, exciting times here that it's a great memory when I'm working on my farm or just sitting with my friends and telling stories of Augusta, the great drama that has occurred," he said.

"And this Tournament is like a magnet. It just draws drama every time. It's almost incredible. And that's what has made this such a great Tournament."

Gary Player was all smiles during his record-tying 50th Tournament appearance.

PAR 3 CONTEST

LEADERS		NEAREST TO HOLE		
PLAYER	SCORE	HOLE PLAYER		INCHES
O'MEARA	5	1 BEEM		2 2
JOHNSON	4	2 GLOVER		2 4
DONALD	4	3 HENRY		1 6
COUPLES	3	4 YANG		2 0
CRENSHAW	3	5 TOMS		0
GOOSEN	3	6 DONALD		3 9
VERPLANK	3	7 SABBATINI		0
HAMILTON	3	8 GRADY		4 5
CINK	3	9 WEIR		4
PETTERSSON	3			

The large scoreboard keeps patrons apprised of who was leading the Par 3 Contest.

All the Mickelson-Woods talk was a prelude to Wednesday's traditional Par 3 Contest and a weather forecast offering something rarely seen since 1997: no rain. Only twice in the past 10 years—in 2001 and 1997—has wet weather not hampered the Tournament.

Mark O'Meara collected his first Par 3 Contest victory, needing just 22 strokes over the 1,060-yard short course.

He edged Zach Johnson and Luke Donald by one stroke on a day when David Toms and Rory Sabbatini recorded the 62nd and 63rd holes-in-one in the 48-year history of the Wednesday event. Toms aced the fifth hole with a 9-iron, and Sabbatini, the seventh hole with a pitching wedge.

"I got a few good breaks out there, but it's a nice score on the Par 3 course," said O'Meara, who also became the 11th different player to win both the Masters Tournament and the Par 3 Contest in his career, although no one's ever done it in the same year.

Past Masters champions Sam Snead and Sandy Lyle have won the Par 3 Contest twice, the only Masters winners to do so.

Jack Nicklaus took a swing at the Par 3 Contest with nothing but fun in mind.

Meanwhile, with clear, cool weather forecast throughout the 72 holes, the 2007 Tournament may provide a picture of what Augusta National will play like—fast and firm from tee to green.

"We had an excellent growing season when we first applied the overseed in September," said Augusta National Golf Club and Masters Tournament Chairman Billy Payne.

"We had a remarkable first few weeks which are critical to the entire process, and we have had a course that looks pretty much today like it did all year."

2007 marked Furman Bisher's (left) 58th Masters.

Masters Major Achievement Award

Fourteen of golf's most respected and admired journalists, each with at least 40 appearances on their résumé, were named recipients of the first Masters Major Achievement Award before the start of the 71st Tournament.

In a Wednesday ceremony at the Press Building, Augusta National Golf Club and Masters Tournament Chairman Billy Payne presented the distinguished journalists with a specially designed plaque made from a hardwood tree that once stood near the second tee.

"The Masters Major Achievement Award was created to recognize those members of the media who have covered 40 or more Masters," said Chairman Payne.

"Their longevity, determination, and talent have played an important role in elevating this Tournament to the position it occupies today. Because of the people we honor today, and others in this room, every golf fan in the world can visualize and describe our beauty, can personally feel and experience the drama and pressure of the second nine on Sunday, and can rejoice in the award of the coveted Green Jacket."

The honorees—with their Masters appearances—include John Derr (62), Furman Bisher (58), Dan Jenkins (57), Al Wester (56), Ron Green Sr. (53), Horace Billings (52), Edwin Pope (51), Dave Moffit (49), Dan Foster (48), Kaye Kessler (44), Nick Seitz (43), Art Spander (41), Dave Kindred (40), and Hubert Mizell (40).

Combined, the 14 journalists have broadcast and written about a total of more than 650 Masters Tournaments spanning eight decades.

Derr attended his first Masters as a journalist in 1935, which was the second Tournament ever played.

"I was not here at the first one," Derr said in his acceptance speech. "And some years later Mr. Roberts called one day and said, 'John, I see you've missed a couple of Masters. Where were you in '34?' And I said, 'Cliff, if they had had any child labor laws in North Carolina, I wouldn't have been here in '35."

All were appreciative of the honor.

"My son reminded me that I have spent, give or take a couple of days, a year of my life covering the Masters," said Ron Green Sr. "I can't imagine many better ways to spend a year of your life than being at the Masters, and I'm deeply indebted to the members of this Club for making that possible and for this award."

"It is we, the writers and announcers who should be thanking Augusta," said Art Spander. "I thank Billy Payne and the administration and everybody else for making the writers always feel wanted here."

Front (left to right): Nick Seitz, David Moffit, Hubert Mizell, Dan Foster, Al Wester, Furman Bisher, Edwin Pope, John Derr, Art Spander. Back: Horace Billings, Dave Kindred, Chairman Billy Payne, Kaye Kessler, Ron Green Sr., Dan Jenkins.

Did You Know?

(MONDAY–WEDNESDAY)

Former Masters winner Raymond Floyd has the sharpest iron shots when it comes to Wednesday's Par 3 Contest. The 1976 Green Jacket winner has won the closest to the flagstick award in the Par 3 Contest a record nine times. Strangely, though, Floyd has won the overall Par 3 Contest competition just once (1990).

Two Masters contestants—Art Wall (1965) and Gay Brewer (1973)—share the course record of seven under par 20 for the Par 3 Contest competition.

The two holes-in-one in 2007, while remarkable, are still three off the record five shot in 2002.

With the invitation of 51 international players to the 2007 Masters, and 50 of them in the final field, there are a record number of foreign-born competitors in the Tournament. The 50 players break the record of 44, which was set in 2005. Since 2003, invitations extended to international players have ranged from 39 to the current 51.

A new era began in 2007, as William Porter Payne became the sixth Chairman of Augusta National Golf Club. Payne joins previous Chairmen Clifford Roberts, William H. Lane, Hord W. Hardin, Jackson T. Stephens, and William W. Johnson.

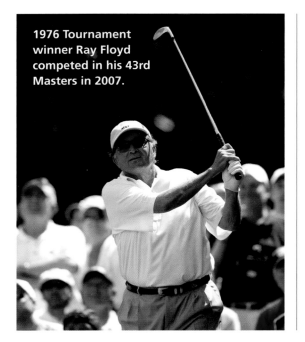

1976 Tournament winner Ray Floyd competed in his 43rd Masters in 2007.

"I think coming into the Tournament we've had as good conditions as I've ever seen," said Rules and Competition Committees Chairman Fred Ridley.

And, said Howell, an Augusta native, those conditions will show both patrons and players how those six holes lengthened prior to 2006 should play like this year.

"You know we still haven't seen it really firm and fast since they made the length changes," said Howell. "So hopefully Mother Nature cooperates and we see it this year."

How the latest rivalry will confront this latest challenge could make for some great golf. ∎

Past champion Mark O'Meara struck deadly short iron shots and needed only 22 strokes to win the Par 3 Contest.

Padraig Harrington

(MONDAY–WEDNESDAY)

It has been seven years in the learning process.

A look at Padraig Harrington's Masters record may not reveal a true contender. Neither does that scoring average of 72.46 strokes per round.

Yes, there's that tie for fifth place in the 2002 Tournament and a tie for 13th in 2004, but mostly the outcome has disappointed him.

Now as he approaches the 2007 Tournament, the Irishman feels his learning curve at Augusta National Golf Club may be heading in the upward direction, but more work remains to be done before he's measured for a Green Jacket.

"I'm only starting to come into a situation where I'm probably a little bit more capable of winning a major," said the Dubliner.

"I definitely think the Masters is the toughest one. It asks the ultimate questions coming down the stretch. There are a lot of shots that have to be absolutely perfect coming down the stretch. The margin for error on the likes of 11, 12, 13, and 15 is very slim."

Harrington said he continues to reshape his game to make his ball trajectory more suited to Augusta National's requirement of high, soft shots.

"The Tournament that I'm thinking about is the Masters, because I think if you can win around here, you can play golf."

Ireland's Padraig Harrington, left, and Scotland's Colin Montgomerie shared on-course time before the Masters.

Left to right: South Africans Trevor Immelman, Gary Player, Tim Clark, and Ernie Els discuss strategy.

Past Par 3 Contest CHAMPIONS

Year	Player	Score
1960	Sam Snead	23
1961	Deane Beman	22
1962	Bruce Crampton	22
1963*	George Bayer	23
1964	Labron Harris Jr.	23
1965	Art Wall	20
1966	Terry Dill	22
1967*	Arnold Palmer	23
1968	Bob Rosburg	22
1969*	Bob Lunn	23
1970	Harold Henning	21
1971*	Dave Stockton	23
1972	Steve Melnyk	23
1973	Gay Brewer	20
1974*	Sam Snead	23
1975*	Isao Aoki	23
1976	Jay Haas	21
1977*	Tom Weiskopf	23
1978*	Lou Graham	22
1979	Joe Inman Jr.	23
1980	Johnny Miller	23
1981	Isao Aoki	22
1982*	Tom Watson	23
1983	Hale Irwin	22
1984	Tommy Aaron	22
1985	Hubert Green	22
1986*	Gary Koch	23
1987	Ben Crenshaw	22
1988	Tsuneyuki Nakajima	24
1989*	Bob Gilder	22
1990	Raymond Floyd	23
1991*	Rocco Mediate	24
1992	Davis Love III	22
1993	Chip Beck	21
1994	Vijay Singh	22
1995*	Hal Sutton	23
1996*	Jay Haas	22
1997*	Sandy Lyle	22
1998	Sandy Lyle	24
1999	Joe Durant	22
2000*	Chris Perry	23
2001	David Toms	22
2002*	Nick Price	22
2003+	Padraig Harrington David Toms	21
2004*	Padraig Harrington	23
2005	Jerry Pate	22
2006	Ben Crane	23
2007	Mark O'Meara	22

*Won in playoff   +Tied

Many preparations took place, including mowing of the fairways, before Tournament play began.

Phil Mickelson's youngest daughter, Sophia, was her dad's caddie during the Par 3 Contest.

2007
Golf Course Changes

No. 11, Par 4, 505 yards: 5 to 7 yards added to the front of the tee. Mow line adjusted about 3 to 5 yards on the golfer's right. Removed grass under the pine trees and replaced it with pine straw on the right side of the fairway.

No. 15, Par 5, 530 yards: 5 to 7 yards added to the front of the tee.

Six-time champion Jack Nicklaus gives his grandson Billy O'Leary a hug during the Par 3 Contest as Gary Player watches.

Patrons always enjoy the panoramic view of the ninth hole during the Par 3 Contest.

Patrons keep track of who is on the practice tee by checking the information boards throughout the day.

THE PRACTICE TEE
LENBY | CAMPBELL C. | BALLESTEROS
YFAIR | CLARKE | HERRON
ENSHAW | CURTIS | SINGH J

2007 Masters Tournament Invitees

Number after each name indicates the basis of qualification. See qualifications on next page.

#Denotes first Masters. *Denotes amateur.

Tommy Aaron (1)
Robert Allenby (Australia) (15, 16, 17)
Stephen Ames (Canada) (5, 10, 14, 16, 17)
Stuart Appleby (Australia) (14, 16, 17)
Aaron Baddeley (Australia) (15, 17)
Severiano Ballesteros (Spain) (1)
Rich Beem (4)
Thomas Bjorn (Denmark) (16)
Gay Brewer Jr. (1)
Bart Bryant (17)
Jack Burke Jr. (1)
Angel Cabrera (Argentina) (10, 16, 17)
Mark Calcavecchia (15)
Chad Campbell (10, 14, 16, 17)
Michael Campbell (New Zealand) (2, 16, 17)
Paul Casey (England) (16, 17)
Billy Casper (1)
K. J. Choi (Korea) (14, 16, 17)
Stewart Cink (10, 14, 16, 17)
Tim Clark (South Africa) (10, 14, 16, 17)
Darren Clarke (N. Ireland) (16)
Charles Coody (1)
Fred Couples (1, 10)
Ben Crane (16)
Ben Crenshaw (1)
Ben Curtis (3, 14)
Chris DiMarco (12, 16, 17)
Luke Donald (England) (13, 14, 16, 17)
#Bradley Dredge (Wales) (16)
Joe Durant (14, 16, 17)
#Johan Edfors (Sweden) (16)
Ernie Els (South Africa) (3, 12, 14, 16, 17)
Nick Faldo (England) (1)
Niclas Fasth (Sweden) (16, 17)
#Kenneth Ferrie (England) (11)
Raymond Floyd (1)

Doug Ford (1)
Fred Funk (5)
Jim Furyk (2, 11, 12, 14, 16, 17)
Sergio Garcia (Spain) (13, 16, 17)
Lucas Glover (14, 16, 17)
Bob Goalby (1)
Retief Goosen (South Africa) (2, 10, 14, 16, 17)
Paul Goydos (17)
#*Julien Guerrier (France) (7)
Todd Hamilton (3)
Padraig Harrington (Ireland) (11, 16, 17)
#J. J. Henry (14)
Tim Herron (14)
Charles Howell III (15, 17)
David Howell (England) (16, 17)
Trevor Immelman (South Africa) (14, 16, 17)
Miguel Angel Jimenez (Spain) (10)
Zach Johnson (14)
#Robert Karlsson (Sweden) (16, 17)
Shingo Katayama (Japan) (16, 17)
Jerry Kelly (14)
#*John Kelly (6-B)
Bernhard Langer (Germany) (1)
Davis Love III (14, 16, 17)
Sandy Lyle (Scotland) (1)
#Troy Matteson (14)
Billy Mayfair (10)
Shaun Micheel (4, 13)
Phil Mickelson (1, 4, 11, 14, 15, 16, 17)
Larry Mize (1)
Colin Montgomerie (Scotland) (11, 16, 17)
Jack Nicklaus (1)
Arron Oberholser (10, 14, 16, 17)
Geoff Ogilvy (Australia) (2, 10, 14, 15, 16, 17)
Nick O'Hern (Australia) (11, 16, 17)
José Maria Olazabal (Spain) (1, 10, 14, 16, 17)

Mark O'Meara (1)
Arnold Palmer (1)
Rod Pampling (Australia) (10, 14, 16, 17)
Tom Pernice Jr. (14)
Carl Pettersson (Sweden) (14, 16, 17)
Gary Player (South Africa) (1)
Ian Poulter (England) (16, 17)
#Brett Quigley (14)
#*Richie Ramsay (Scotland) (6-A)
John Rollins (15, 17)
Justin Rose (England) (17)
Rory Sabbatini (South Africa) (14, 16)
Adam Scott (Australia) (13, 14, 16, 17)
#Jeev Milkha Singh (India) (16, 17)
Vijay Singh (Fiji) (1, 4, 10, 11, 14, 15, 16, 17)
Jeff Sluman (11)
Craig Stadler (1)
Henrik Stenson (Sweden) (15, 16, 17)
Steve Stricker (11, 14, 17)
#Hideto Tanihara (Japan)
Vaughn Taylor (14)
David Toms (14, 16, 17)
Scott Verplank (10, 14)
#Camilo Villegas (Colombia) (14)
#*Casey Watabu (8)
Tom Watson (1)
Mike Weir (Canada) (1, 10, 11, 14, 16, 17)
Lee Westwood (England) (16)
#Brett Wetterich (14, 16, 17)
#Dean Wilson (14)
#*Dave Womack (9)
Tiger Woods (1, 2, 3, 4, 10, 14, 15, 16, 17)
Ian Woosnam (Wales) (1)
#Y. E. Yang (Korea) (16, 17)
Fuzzy Zoeller (1)

How They Qualified

1 Masters Tournament champions (lifetime)

2 U.S. Open champions (honorary, noncompeting after five years)

3 British Open champions (honorary, noncompeting after five years)

4 PGA champions (honorary, noncompeting after five years)

5 Winners of The Players Championship (2005 and 2006)

6 Current U.S. Amateur champion (6-A) (honorary, non-competing after one year) and the runner-up (6-B) to the current U.S. Amateur champion

7 Current British Amateur champion (honorary, noncompeting after one year)

8 Current U.S. Amateur Public Links champion

9 Current U.S. Mid-Amateur champion

10 The first 16 players, including ties, in the 2006 Masters Tournament

11 The first eight players, including ties, in the 2006 U.S. Open Championship

12 The first four players, including ties, in the 2006 British Open Championship

13 The first four players, including ties, in the 2006 PGA Championship

14 The 40 leaders on the Final Official PGA Tour Money List for 2006

15 The 10 leaders on the Official PGA Tour Money List published during the week prior to the 2007 Masters Tournament

16 The 50 leaders on the Final Official World Golf Ranking for 2006

17 The 50 leaders on the Official World Golf Ranking published during the week prior to the 2007 Masters Tournament

The Masters Committee, at its discretion, also invites international players not otherwise qualified.

Players practice on Augusta National's fast, undulating greens.

Rose, Wetterich Take Different Paths to Lead

— ❚❚❚ —

Brett Wetterich used lessons from past champions and Justin Rose used past experiences at Augusta National Golf Club to take the first-round lead with scores of 69. They were the only players in the field to break 70.

When England's Justin Rose and America's Brett Wetterich came to the 2007 Tournament, they knew experience would be a necessary tool for success.

The average number of years it has taken a past Masters champion to win his first Green Jacket is six. And only 22 of the previous 42 champions have managed to come in under that figure.

Rose and Wetterich learned that lesson in different ways, they said, after posting three-under-par 69s, the only sub-70 scores on a day when cool temperatures and light breezes sent players reaching for the aspirin bottle at day's end.

The field scoring average of 76.19 strokes per player, the 13th-highest first-round total in history, attested to that fact. Rose's round was bogey-free, the only one of the day.

Two players—David Howell and David Toms—shot 70, and five players—2006 runner-up Tim Clark, Augusta native Vaughn Taylor, former PGA champion Rich Beem, and U.S. Ryder Cup team members Zach Johnson and J. J. Henry—were at 71.

Five players were at even par, while 12 finished in the 80s.

Defending champion Phil Mickelson suffered through a first nine of 40 and shot 76, largely thanks to two birdies on the last four holes, and Tiger Woods shot 73, bogeying his final two holes.

"I got off to a poor start and I was five over after seven," said Mickelson, who placed a double bogey, four bogeys, and one birdie on his card in that opening stretch.

"I don't feel I've driven myself out of it, as even par is going to be in the hunt tomorrow."

Woods, a keen student of Augusta National's nuances, was disappointed by his finish and needed to regroup.

"I threw away a good round of golf," he said of the bogey-bogey finish. "I've got to organize a few things. I had it right there. Then I threw it away."

Yet Wetterich, a rookie, used his pre-Tournament warm-up rounds as learning

Justin Rose hit nine of 14 fairways but needed a mere 20 putts to shoot a 69 and share the lead.

tools that helped him card five birdies and two bogeys for his share of the lead.

Without his calculated planning, said the 33-year-old Jupiter, Florida, resident, he might not have hit 12 of 18 greens in regulation and taken just 27 putts over the sloping, fast-putting surfaces.

"You know, I got some good advice from people and that was awfully helpful," said the 2006 EDS Byron Nelson Championship winner.

"I got to play with Mr. [Ray] Floyd on Tuesday and he told me an awful lot about the golf course and little different putts that in my mind they have to go right [but] that are dead straight—just little things like that.

He gave me a little bit of a chipping lesson, which was awfully helpful."

Wetterich also played with another Masters champion, Larry Mize, on Monday, and "he gave me a lot of information as well."

While Wetterich drew on knowledge of the golf course from past champions, Rose drew his lessons from painful past experience.

In 2004 the then 23-year-old fired off rounds of 67 and 71 for a 138. He led the field after 18 and 36 holes. But a letdown in the third round—the tally was 81—pushed him to a tie for 20th place heading into the final round. Rose rebounded with a

This tee shot at No. 17 set up Brett Wetterich's fifth birdie of the day.

one-under-par 71, and his 290 aggregate was good for a tie for 22nd.

But, said the London resident, he realized that the Masters requires the utmost of your attention and the best of your abilities each and every shot, each and every day.

"I think it's certainly something that I can learn a lot from, that experience, no doubt," he said three years later.

"I think experience is generally what makes players better and better as they go throughout their career. It's a very positive one as I look back at it. Sometimes you learn more from situations that go badly than when things go well. So I learned a lot about the golf course that particular day and I learned a lot about how you've got to really pace yourself during the week."

Despite his score, Rose's round was statistically misleading in some ways.

He hit only five of 18 greens in regulation and ranked tied for 86th among the 96 players, one less than when the day started

U.S. Amateur Public Links Championship winner Casey Watabu of Hawaii was one of five amateurs in the field.

David Toms and his caddie, Scott Gneiser, reading putts in the first round.

What They're Saying
(ROUND ONE)

I would say it is quite playable, but the scores aren't that great looking at the board. People have done it time and time again around here. If you start going at pins when you're two or three over par, you'll get punished. You have to take your medicine and wait until you get a chance and try and take it.

 —Ian Poulter, speaking about the over-par scores showing up in the first round

It was great to see Arnie. But the moment of silence for Mr. [Byron] Nelson was very special. The moment of silence brought tears to my eyes.

 —Billy Mayfair regarding the ceremony honoring the late Byron Nelson, and Arnold Palmer debuting as Honorary Starter

It's a little nerve-wracking watching the Tournament your whole life and then playing in it.

 —Hawaiian Dean Wilson, a first-time Masters participant, after shooting a 75

This is the fastest I've seen the greens since I've played them here. And this is my 12th Masters.

 —Scott Verplank on the difficulty of the greens

Standards display hole scores.

THRU 15	
ALLENBY	7
WETTERICH	2
WESTWOOD	6

HOLE NO. 1

Par 4; 455 yards

Name: Tea Olive

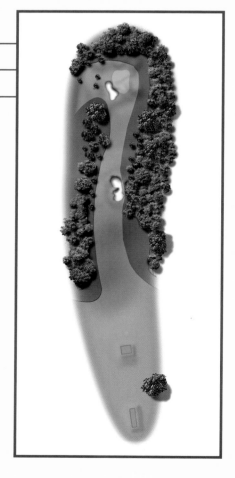

The 455-yard, par-4 first hole took its toll on the 96-player field in the first round. As one of six holes that were lengthened 15 to 20 yards prior to the 2006 Masters, Tea Olive has found new bite and is yielding its share of over-par numbers. In the first round of 2006, the hole played to an average of 4.388 shots per player, yielding only five birdies. In 2007, the hole played even tougher, averaging 4.489. It yielded two birdies, 36 bogeys, five double bogeys, and one triple bogey. Only past champion Vijay Singh and two-time U.S. Open champion Retief Goosen were able to record birdies.

because past champion Ian Woosnam withdrew due to a back injury.

Rose hit nine of the 14 generous fairways for a 64.29 percent accuracy that was 42nd best, but putted lights out on the greens.

He needed only 20 putts over the 18 holes and led the field.

And his short game, a fundamental requirement in the Masters, was superb.

"My short game was unbelievable today," he said, "and that's why I managed to shoot such a good score and play a bogey-free round.

"Up and down well, controlled my chips well, managed to control the track and trajectory on them. Also I put myself in spots where you could up-and-down the ball."

Rose chalks up his first-round smartness to both lessons learned from 2004 about the importance of course management in the Masters *and* maturity in his game.

Those two factors, he said, are worth their weight in gold around these parts.

How much better a player is he now than in 2004? Rose was asked.

"I think a lot—a lot better, a lot better," he said frankly.

"I've been working hard on my game over the last two or three years, so I hope that that alone makes me a better player. I feel comfortable in my golf game, and obviously golf is a game of confidence and I feel quite confident, too."

For every confident Justin Rose, there were a dozen or more uncomfortable players scattered across the rest of the field.

Even David Howell, who was tied for third place with Toms, wasn't brimming with confidence despite an opening 70.

"I didn't come in today with an awful lot of confidence from my play before this

Signaling his position as the Honorary Starter for 2007, Arnold Palmer's name stands alone at the first tee.

With a trademark thumbs-up gesture, Arnold Palmer was pleased with his historic tee shot.

Shot of the Day
(ROUND ONE)

It was a shot viewed, perhaps, by more patrons than any other single shot of the first round of the Masters, and if it had no direct bearing on the Tournament's outcome, it was very significant to the traditions of the event founded by Bobby Jones and Clifford Roberts. Arnold Palmer, a four-time Masters champion, became the seventh Honorary Starter in Tournament history. Palmer's opening tee shot, his first in the position since his competitive retirement in 2004, came on a nippy spring morning and was warmly accepted by tens of thousands of patrons who rose early to see the 7:45 A.M. ceremony.

Did You Know?
(ROUND ONE)

While it's always good to lead a Masters after the fourth round, if you lead or share the lead at the end of the previous rounds enough times, chances are you will win a Green Jacket sometime in your career. Arnold Palmer, for example, led or shared the lead 14 times in his Masters career and earned four titles. Jack Nicklaus, winner of six Masters, is next in line with 13.

Horton Smith, Gene Sarazen, and Fuzzy Zoeller are the only players to win in their first attempt, while Mark O'Meara took the longest time to win his first Masters (1998), 15 years after his first appearance.

Subpar golf, nearly of the double-digit kind, has been needed more often than not since 1990 if you expect to be a Masters winner. In the prior 17 Masters Tournaments, it took a score of 279 or better 14 times to claim a Green Jacket regardless of the weather conditions.

Heading into the 2007 Masters there have been a total of 1,069 different players competing at Augusta National Golf Club, stretching from "A" (Tommy Aaron) to "Z" (Richard Zokol). Ten fathers and sons and 25 sets of brothers have received invitations.

What They're Writing

(ROUND ONE)

At 7:38 A.M., on a cool morning as radiant as his smile, Arnold Palmer emerged from the clubhouse at the Augusta National Golf Club and made his way toward the first tee, a pale-blue sweater on his back and Gene Sarazen on his mind.

He had made the walk many times before—50 in all since 1955, when he first played in the Masters—and the entrance always seems to be the same. Heads turn. Necks strain. Crowds part, almost biblically. This was no different.

Thousands began streaming toward the first tee when the gates opened at 7:30 A.M., waiting to see a slice of tradition be recaptured by a man who brought that and much more to the Masters. "Looked like 20,000 people flooding through that gate," Palmer would say later.

They came to see the King, make no mistake. What they got, though, was a re-birth. Perhaps even a small measure of history.

—Gerry Dulac, Pittsburgh Post-Gazette

She was waiting for him in the gallery, right after he walked off the seventh green, the same hole where he had flubbed an easy chip shot a few minutes before. Amy Mickelson threw her arms around her husband, Phil, and hugged him tightly.

It was that kind of opening day at the Masters on Thursday. A lot of players could have used a whole lot of hugs after what they went through at Augusta National Golf Club and Mickelson was one of them.

The first ball he hit as the defending champion hit a tree and dropped straight to the ground.

From then on, it was all downhill, at least for a while. Through seven holes, Mickelson was five over par, but he pulled himself together after getting that hug from his wife. After dropping to six over through 14 holes, he birdied two of the last four to wind up with a four-over 76 that could have been a lot worse.

—Thomas Bonk, Los Angeles Times

On Monday afternoon, a person inside the Augusta National clubhouse gave a player's badge to someone from India. That had never happened before.

On Thursday afternoon, the white leader boards throughout the course bore a familiar name and a puzzling initial. J. Singh was tied for first place at the Masters, at 3 under par.

"I'm pretty sure this will be a very big story in the newspapers back there," Jeev Milkha Singh said after he finished.

He was relaxed and smiling, a loose-jointed 35-year-old who speaks with little accent. He has a caddie from Japan, Ippei Fujimoro, who speaks far less English than Singh does. They spent much of Thursday speaking with their hands, as they tried to decipher the Augusta greens.

—Mark Whicker, Orange County Register

A 69, three under par, enabled Justin Rose to take a share of the lead in the first round of the Masters on a day when few seemed to want it. Only Brett Wetterich, the American who was making his debut in this event, was able to match the tall Englishman.

As the sun began to slip behind the tall pines, David Howell, Rose's fellow Englishman, came in with a 70, and Luke Donald, a third Englishman and one of Howell's Europe teammates in the victorious Ryder Cup last autumn, had a 73. He was joined by Tiger Woods, who dropped shots at his last two holes.

It is appropriate that a man with a surname such as Rose should be leading the field over a course laid out on what was once a nursery, but it is also a surprise. A back injury has prevented Rose from playing competitively since the end of February and he has spent much of the past five weeks doing rehabilitation exercises for his back.

—John Hopkins, Times of London

England's Justin Rose recorded a bogey-free 69, including par here at No. 15, to tie Brett Wetterich for the first-round lead.

week," said the Englishman of a round that included a little bit of everything: one eagle, three birdies, one bogey, and one double bogey.

"[I was] a little nervy on the first tee wondering how the day was going to go. I basically went out there to try to manage my game as well as I can and not make any major errors and blow myself out of the Tournament."

For many other players the first round left them speechless or shaking their heads in dismay.

Course conditions—firm and fast fairways and greens for the first time in six years—was the likely reason.

Some were crestfallen, such as Ernie Els, who owns six top-10 finishes in 13 Tournaments, after a six-over-par 78. His round was punctuated by a six-over-par start on his first nine holes, including a double bogey at No. 1, and additional putting woes.

"It was terrible on the front nine, starting with a double and then three-putting on two for another bogey," he said dejectedly. "It was a difficult day, a very tough day. If you mishit a shot today, you really paid the penalty."

With the weather forecast calling for dry but cool conditions, the likelihood that the course will remain firm and dry and therefore unforgiving, is high.

It could create some interesting moments in the second, third, and final rounds, said two-time champions José Maria Olazabal and Ben Crenshaw.

"There is no way we are going to have low scores if the weather stays dry like this and Augusta National wants to have the greens firm," said the Spaniard.

"You feel like the course is going to get you somewhere," said Crenshaw. "It doesn't matter who you are." ▌

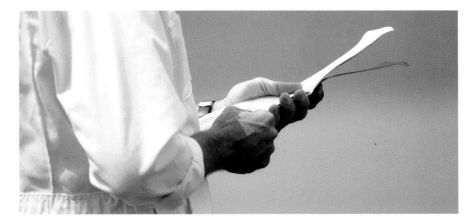

Making sure their numbers are correct, caddies constantly consult yardage books.

An errant drive at the 15th hole cost Brett Wetterich his second bogey on the day.

Arnold Palmer

(ROUND ONE)

He came rolling around the front of the stately white Clubhouse in a golf cart headed toward one of the most memorable days in his golfing career.

Let it be written that at 7:10 A.M. on April 5, 2007, Arnold Daniel Palmer, four-time Masters winner, was making his way to the practice tee at Augusta National Golf Club.

The official start of the Masters was less than an hour away, but on this day there would be a different role for one of the Tournament's most beloved champions.

Three years after his retirement from the Masters' competitive arena, Palmer was to resume a time-honored tradition as the Honorary Starter, a role previously assumed by the likes of Jock Hutchinson (1963–1973), Fred McLeod (1963–1976), Byron Nelson (1981–2001), Gene Sarazen (1981–1999), Ken Venturi (1983), and Sam Snead (1984–2002).

It's hard, however, to break a routine that's been your life for many, many years.

So he went to the practice tee wearing a light blue cashmere sweater, a navy blue shirt, and gray slacks, the epitome of fashion sense as always, and began working his way through his golf bag, short irons first and then longer clubs.

He was laughing and dodging the question of nerves.

"Oh, am I nervous?" he said, his voice belying the noncommittal answer.

Fourteen practice shots later, including five of them drives lashed down the practice tee in typical Palmer fashion, he was ready to go on his grandest stage, the first tee at Augusta National.

"Put me in, coach," he said, taking up the position.

With his warm-up complete at 7:23 A.M., he signed a few autographs and walked the short distance through the Clubhouse, holding hands with his wife, Kit, and talking with Masters Chairman Billy Payne.

Routine. That's all it was. Routine, he said. He'd prepared the same way for all these years, but today was different. Or was it?

"He was quite relaxed last night," said Kit. "He slept well and has been looking forward to it. He's not overly nervous."

But Palmer's caddie, David Chapman, was. "I was so nervous last night I couldn't sleep," he confessed.

As his 7:45 A.M. tee time ticked closer, Palmer peeked out the Clubhouse door, watching patrons encircle the first tee in large numbers, all of them wanting to see their favorite Masters champion begin the Tournament.

"Isn't that something?" Palmer said to an audience of Augusta National officials.

"I've never seen anything like it," said Kit Palmer.

Patrons were lined up 10 deep from the first tee for nearly 100 yards, each hoping to grab a glimpse of a Masters tradition.

Masters caddies stopped in their tracks to soak in the moment. So did a few of the early players, including Ben Crenshaw, a historian who knew a magic moment when he saw one.

"All of us wanted this to be his decision," said Crenshaw on his way to the putting green.

"I watched it just before I had to go to the practice tee. It's great for the history of the Masters. A lot of us can't believe this moment has come, that Arnold's now an Honorary Starter."

Where, Crenshaw mused, did the time go?

Out the door Palmer went to warm, loud applause, an introduction on the first tee by Chairman Payne, and then came the moment of truth.

The Masters legend drew back the driver, brought it to the ball in his typical slashing style, and watched it head down the left-center of the first fairway with a slight draw that carried it into the left rough.

"There was some excitement in the air," he said afterward, but no butterflies.

"I did something last night that I haven't done in a long time. I went to bed at, what, about 10:00, 10:30, and I slept until 5:00 this morning without moving, and I don't ever do that."

Maybe it was the strong conviction of the decision to become the seventh Honorary Starter in Tournament history that let him sleep peacefully.

"I think the time had come," said the 77-year-old, who had weighed his option as an Honorary Starter carefully the past three years. "My competitive golf is done."

But the competitor in Palmer remains and will forever be so.

He wanted to soak in the warm applause from the thousands of appreciative patrons on hand to see his tee shot kick off the Masters.

He wanted that shot to be Palmeresque—long with a slight draw into the fairway—and it was indeed mostly that.

It was also a time of handling the emotions of the moment for the western Pennsylvania native.

"It is a great thrill for me and an honor," he said afterward.

"I was thinking back [to] when I went to Wake Forest and I used to watch the Masters and think about coming here, and whoever thought that 60 years later, here we are."

That mixture of emotions—some raw and unchecked—did surface before, during, and after his tee shot, Palmer said.

"Certainly there's a lot of emotion and a lot of feeling for Augusta," he said, reflecting on the special place Augusta National and the Masters hold in his heart.

"You know, I have—well, what I'm thinking about is the years I first came here in 1955 and shortly after that, I got to know Cliff Roberts and Bob Jones, and for me and all the things that ranked in my life: my father, being in golf; and then in '58, it really started happening when I won. And Dwight Eisenhower was president of the United States and Cliff Roberts came out and said that the president wanted to play golf Monday morning. So that kind of kicked things off. That got the whole thing going."

Now, as he nears his 78th birthday in September, Palmer's treasure trove of memories ranges from handshakes with Masters patrons to dinners with presidents, kings, and other heads of state; and now there's a new chapter in his scrapbook: Honorary Starter at the Masters.

Surrounded by thousands of patrons, Arnold Palmer began the 2007 Tournament.

Former PGA Championship winner Rich Beem needed just 24 putts to shoot a 71.

Sweden's Henrik Stenson was one of five players at even par after the first round.

Round One LEADERS			1	2	3	4	5	6	7	8	9	Out	10	11	12	13	14	15	16	17	18	In	Rd1	Total
Pos.	Player	Par	4	5	4	3	4	3	4	5	4	36	4	4	3	5	4	5	3	4	4	36	72	
T1	J. Rose		4	5	3	3	3	3	4	5	4	34	4	4	3	5	3	5	3	4	4	35	69	−3
T1	B. Wetterich		4	6	4	3	4	3	3	5	3	35	3	4	3	4	4	6	3	3	4	34	69	−3
T3	D. Howell		4	5	4	5	4	3	3	4	4	36	3	4	3	5	5	3	3	4	4	34	70	−2
T3	D. Toms		4	5	4	3	5	3	4	5	3	36	4	3	3	5	3	5	3	4	4	34	70	−2
T5	R. Beem		5	5	4	3	4	3	4	4	3	35	5	5	2	3	4	5	3	4	5	36	71	−1
T5	T. Clark		4	5	4	3	4	2	4	5	5	36	4	4	3	5	4	5	3	4	3	35	71	−1
T5	J. J. Henry		4	4	4	2	4	4	5	5	4	36	4	4	3	5	5	4	3	4	3	35	71	−1
T5	Z. Johnson		5	4	4	3	4	3	4	4	4	35	5	4	3	4	4	4	4	4	4	36	71	−1
T5	V. Taylor		4	5	4	3	4	3	4	4	5	36	4	5	2	5	4	3	4	4	4	35	71	−1

Learning lessons from past travails, Justin Rose managed his game and score superbly in the first round.

Topped with flags from each player's country, the Masters scoreboard keeps patrons up-to-date on the Tournament.

Clark, Wetterich Make Field Take Notice

III

Under firm, fast conditions, 2006 runner-up Tim Clark shot a second 71 and Brett Wetterich shot a 73 for a two-under-par 142 total after 36 holes. They held a one-stroke lead over Augusta's Vaughn Taylor.

A year ago Tim Clark came to his fifth Masters without much fanfare. A glimpse at his prior Augusta National record, which included two missed cuts, a tie for 39th, and a tie for 13th, wouldn't have raised an eyebrow among casual golf fans.

This was a man who is known as a good iron player and a very good putter, but a relatively short hitter by today's standards.

That he finished second to Phil Mickelson in the 2006 Tournament surprised some. Maybe it was an anomaly, they may have wondered.

Now as the Masters reached the midway point with Clark tied for the lead with Brett Wetterich, the 5-foot-7, 165-pound Clark has made people sit up and take notice.

Not that that's anything new for the Durban-born player.

"Well, I guess no one's ever picked me to do well anywhere," he said bluntly after posting a four-birdie, one-bogey, one-double-bogey round of 71 and a 36-hole total of two-under-par 142.

"I've had a third at the PGA, a third at the U.S. Open, and a second here, so my major record is pretty decent to people who haven't won a major."

There is nothing to indicate a reason for Clark's recent Masters success since turning professional in 1998, although injuries have halted his progress at times.

Clark won twice on the Nationwide Tour and three times on the PGA European Tour since turning pro. His best money ranking on the PGA Tour is 21st in 2005. He was 32nd on the list last year.

Yet even Clark wonders if the respect will come only if he slips into a Green Jacket one day.

"Even after yesterday [when] I was on the leader board, no one mentioned me," he said. "Everyone was looking at everyone else to do well. You know, maybe that will just give me a little more incentive to go out there, and [it] probably will take me winning a major tournament for people to sort of recognize me."

If his golf remains at the high standard it

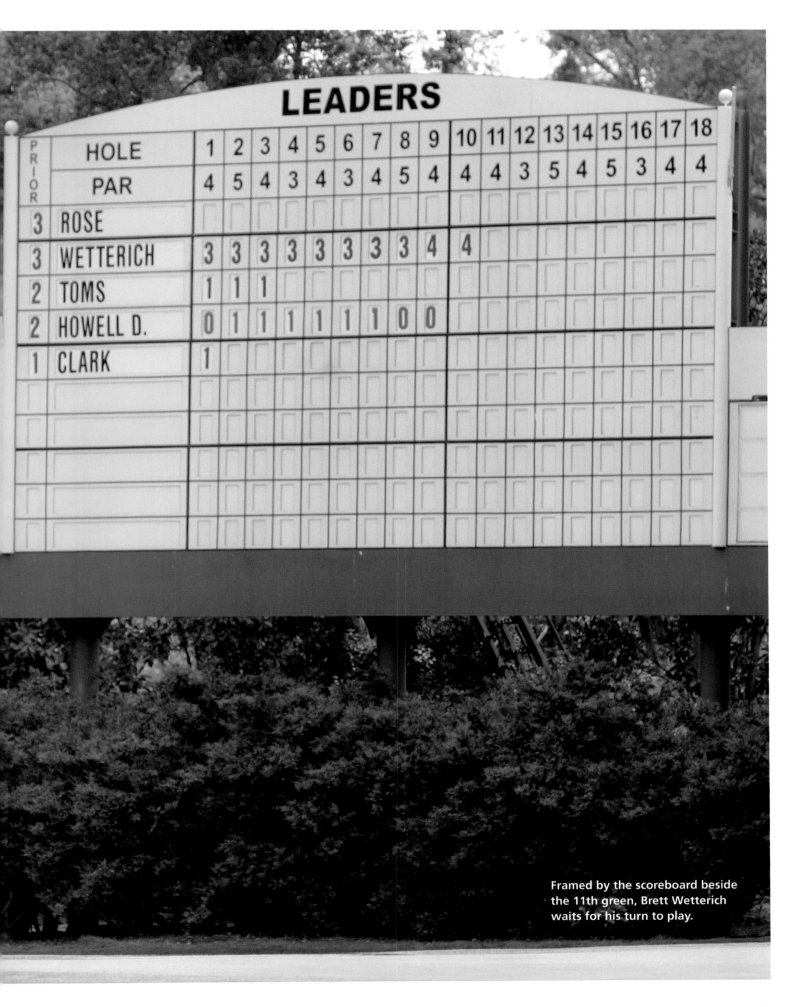

LEADERS

PRIOR	HOLE	1	2	3	4	5	6	7	8	9	10	11	12	13	14	15	16	17	18
	PAR	4	5	4	3	4	3	4	5	4	4	4	3	5	4	5	3	4	4
3	ROSE																		
3	WETTERICH	3	3	3	3	3	3	3	3	4	4								
2	TOMS	1	1	1															
2	HOWELL D.	0	1	1	1	1	1	1	0	0									
1	CLARK	1																	

Framed by the scoreboard beside the 11th green, Brett Wetterich waits for his turn to play.

A second-straight one-under-par 71 gave Tim Clark a share of the 36-hole lead.

has been at Augusta National, Clark's time may come sooner than later.

Clark, as well as Wetterich, survived another tough day. The weather remained dry, and the fast greens remained consistent.

That enabled players to make dramatic moves up and down the leader board.

Augusta native Vaughn Taylor shot 72 and stood at 143, one under par, in third place. His three-birdie, three-bogey round left him as the only other player under par.

Four more players, including past champion Vijay Singh (71), Jerry Kelly (69), Zach Johnson (73), and first-round coleader Justin Rose (75), were at level par 144.

Kelly's round, one of only three sub-70 scores on the day along with Padraig Harrington (68) and Paul Casey (68), was not indicative of the difficult conditions.

But Kelly, Harrington, and Casey all made significant moves up the leader board.

Kelly moved from a tie for 28th after the first round to a tie for fourth, and his position would have been even better if not for a bogey on the final hole. Harrington jumped from a tie for 59th to a tie for eighth; and Casey's 68, which included an eagle at No. 2, moved him up 60 spots, to tie for 15th, at the end of the day.

Beyond those seven players at even par or better, the field was packed tightly.

Six players were at 145, including Geoff Ogilvy; past Masters winners Mike Weir, Craig Stadler, and Woods were at three-over-par 147. The Masters' first player from India, Jeev Milkha Singh, also stood at three over.

Vaughn Taylor watches his delicate pitch shot over the bunker trickle toward the 16th hole and narrowly miss falling in for a birdie, prompting an emotional reaction.

What They're Writing

(ROUND TWO)

Tiger Woods plopped two shots into the water Friday. He made bogeys on six of his first 12 holes, sent wayward drives sailing all over the Georgia landscape and threatened to leave so much distance between himself and the leaders, he might not matter on the weekend.

But when the haze lifted on another daunting day at Augusta National, there stood Woods—lurking five shots off the pace.

Woods stitched together a second-round 74, reaching the halfway point in the thick of contention at the Masters. Tim Clark (71) and Brett Wetterich (73) shared the 36-hole lead at 2-under, one shot ahead of Augusta native Vaughn Taylor. Vijay Singh headlined a quartet of players at even-par, two shots back.

That was no misprint: Only three players stood below par for the tournament after another day of shifting winds and speedy greens. The wind is expected to blow more vigorously the next two days, which could create a furious scramble for the green jacket.

—Ron Kroichick, San Francisco Chronicle

Although Augusta National is rightly regarded as the cathedral of American golf, the hush which surrounded yesterday morning's play as the second round of the 71st Masters unfolded was better suited to a church sermon than the action at a major championship.

Once the course echoed with gasps and roars from the patrons as eagles followed birdies. The toughening of the test to the point where 82 of the 96 players in the field started the second round over par, however, suggested most of the players now eschew boldness. On top of added length and firm and fast conditions, those who went out before lunch also found the weather brisk to the point of chilly.

—Mike Aitken, Scotsman

Tiger Woods surfaced from two trips to the water to hand in an extraordinary 74 which left him on three over par at the half-way stage of the 71st Masters. Playing in the same group, Paul Casey enjoyed a remarkable comeback—he followed an opening 79 with a 68—to go into the weekend on precisely the same mark.

"No-one's going anywhere," said Woods, as he scanned the afternoon leaderboard and saw that three over was only five behind.

By the end of the day, Brett Wetterich and Tim Clark were sharing the top spot on two under. Justin Rose, who had been alongside Wetterich overnight dropped three shots but is still thoroughly well-placed at level par.

—Lewine Mair, London Telegraph

Stuart Appleby likened his joust with Augusta National to a prizefight after playing himself to within three shots of the lead with a second round 70.

Appleby was out on his feet, but still punching, as he prepared to chase leaders Brett Wetterich and Tim Clark into the championship rounds.

"Augusta is a tough opponent with a very good record against the best in the business," he said. "You can't relax for a moment. You have to keep moving, use your jab and stay light on your feet. If not, you're going to be knocked out."

—Bernie Pramberg, News Limited *(Australia)*

"I turned a 90 into a 74 today," Woods said of an inconsistent four-birdie, six-bogey day. "Yesterday I threw away a good round and today I salvaged a bad one, so I'm still in the game."

Phil Mickelson rebounded from an opening 76 with a 73 and stood at 149, seven shots behind Wetterich and Clark.

The cut came at eight-over-par 152, the highest score since 1982, with 60 players

Vijay Singh's short game was up and down, but the past champion was able to shoot a 71.

enjoying a weekend chance to win a Green Jacket.

In all, 10 past champions prepared for two more rounds. They included Fred Couples, who made his 23rd consecutive cut; 55-year-old Ben Crenshaw; Sandy Lyle; Mickelson; José Maria Olazabal; Vijay Singh; Stadler; Weir; Woods; and 55-year-old Fuzzy Zoeller.

There were, however, notable casualties: past winners Seve Ballesteros, Ray Floyd, Bernhard Langer, Mark O'Meara, Larry Mize, Gary Player, and Tom Watson, as well as the likes of Ernie Els (78–76—154) and 2005 runner-up Chris DiMarco (75–78—153). No amateurs made the cut.

All of that ebb and flow of Tournament action did nothing to detract from either Clark or Wetterich's pace-setting play.

Clark overcame a double bogey at the 455-yard, par-4 fifth, where he lost his drive into the right trees, by holing a putt from off the green for par at the 18th to retain his share of the lead. He made birdies at Nos. 3, 8, 10, and 13 on the day.

"You know I was just trying to bring home the round," he said of the adventures at the last hole. "I thought I did pretty well to get home to one-under. This course is just playing so tough right now."

Wetterich, who is playing in his first Masters, kept firm to his game plan of not wanting to make a big number.

"I wanted to make a lot of pars," he said of his philosophy.

Two-time champion Ben Crenshaw wasn't happy finishing bogey-bogey-bogey for his 74.

"You always hear the great players say that pars are great in majors. I was just going out there to try to make as many as I could and I did pretty good for 14 holes, and then had a few hiccups, but kind of gathered myself and had a good 17th and 18th hole."

The Ohio-born Wetterich did, indeed, follow his plan of playing smartly.

Shot of the Day
(ROUND TWO)

In two previous Masters appearances England's Paul Casey has never had much success on the 575-yard, par-5 second hole. He's made only one birdie at the downhill hole in seven previous attempts. But during Friday's second round Casey made up for that in a big way. He hit the green in two and then holed a 40-footer for an eagle. That quick start was just the momentum he needed for the day. After opening with a 79—and facing the possibility of missing the 36-hole cut—Casey shot a four-under-par 68, and his total of three-over-par 147 kept him in the hunt for the Green Jacket over the weekend.

He parred the first eight holes, birdied the ninth with a 25-foot putt, added five more pars, and then three-putted both the 15th and 16th holes for bogeys. Two more pars, including an up-and-down from eight feet at the next-to-last hole, brought him a round of 73, which included 15 pars.

"I definitely am playing a little less aggressive than I normally play for sure," said the 33-year-old.

Caution also was Taylor's path to his even-par round, which left him one shot back heading into the third round.

There were three birdies and three bogeys on his card, and that was just fine with him.

"I feel like I'm putting well and I feel like I'm swinging well, and, you know, speed on the greens is really key," he said of his second Masters.

"You definitely have to hit it in the right spots on the greens as well. So hopefully that's an advantage for me."

Paul Casey's best finish at the Masters was T6 in 2004.

Coleader Brett Wetterich knew full well the dangers of this tee shot at No. 12.

With 24 players within five shots of the lead, two rounds remaining, and cold, windy weather facing the field before the Tournament ends, it all shapes up as a thrilling windup to the first major of the year.

Beware, said the players, of the days ahead because it may be the most difficult they have ever seen here. The field scoring average has been well above par through the first two rounds. It was 76.19 in the first round and 75.63 in the second.

"You can never count anybody out around this place especially," said Kelly, knowing that past champions such as Vijay Singh, Woods, Mickelson, and Olazabal are well aware that good, solid rounds a few under par on the weekend will surely help them improve their positions.

"If it stays like this, there won't be any scores under par," predicted 1992 winner Fred Couples.

HOLE OF THE DAY

(ROUND TWO)

HOLE NO. 12

Par 3; 155 yards

Name: Golden Bell

This is always one of the most dangerous holes at the Masters. And during the second round it was no different. The field averaged 3.447 strokes per player, and the hole ranked the third most difficult. Two players had particularly interesting results there. Paul Casey nearly holed his tee shot and made a birdie en route to a 68, equaling the low round of the day. Then there was Tiger Woods, who hit his tee shot into the bank and watched it roll into the water, dropped with penalty, hit his third 20 feet behind the hole, and then holed a treacherous downhill putt, saving a bogey from potential disaster. He shot a 74.

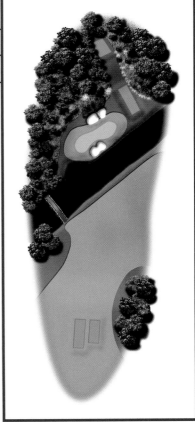

Brett Wetterich shot a 73 and ended the day tied for the 36-hole lead.

Did You Know?

(ROUND TWO)

Although there were 18 first-time participants in the Masters this year, it was not a record. The most rookies lately came in 1962 and 1966, when there were 22. In the second year of the Masters, there were 23.

A record continued for Fred Couples. Couples has made the cut in all 23 of his Masters appearances. He shot rounds of 76–76—152. His mark also tied the record held by Gary Player (1959–1982) for the most consecutive cuts made.

While Couples continued his streak, Ernie Els's mark of 11 consecutive cuts ended. Els totaled 154 and missed playing on the weekend for the first time since 1995, which was his second Masters.

Brett Wetterich has become only the sixth Masters rookie to lead or colead after the first and second rounds. He joins Horton Smith (1934), Lloyd Mangrum (1940), Billy Joe Patton (1954), Bert Yancey (1967), and Chris DiMarco (2001).

There have been only two years since the 36-hole cut was instituted that had higher scores than today's 152 strokes. In 1982 the cut was at 154, and in 1966 it was 153.

"It's windy and long. If you get a guy who is five or six over and shoots three or four under, they will have a good shot on Sunday."

"Patience," said Johnson, "is of the utmost importance."

Patience might as well be Vijay Singh's middle name.

Through two rounds he has eight birdies and eight bogeys along with 20 pars. The Fijian has three-putted only once.

He is cautiously optimistic and hopeful to be in the hunt for a second Masters title.

"Just playing solid golf, and my putting is decent," he said.

Solid golf will be necessary to win, judging from the firm and fast conditions on display this week. It may even become a historic weekend in the record books.

Keep in mind that in the past 53 years, even par or higher scores have won a Green Jacket only three times.

In 1954, Sam Snead and Ben Hogan tied at 289 before Snead won the ensuing playoff. In 1956, Jack Burke shot 289, one over par, and in 1966 Jack Nicklaus won with an even-par 288.

It could happen again. ∎

Padraig Harrington's bunker shot at the second hole provided the second of three straight birdies and gave him a 68 for the round.

Jerry Kelly
(ROUND TWO)

Springtime in Georgia, particularly in Augusta, is a panorama of blooming flowers.

It is the sight of dogwoods and azaleas punctuating the Masters air.

Yes, there is rain, but that only makes the flowers brighter.

What lit up Jerry Kelly's eyes, though, was talk of the cold facing the field for the third round.

He's a Wisconsin guy.

His Madison home is a place where bitter temperatures are the norm and where you know it's summer when the snow gets a little slushy.

With the weather for the third round predicted to be in the mid-30s at dawn, a high in the mid-50s, and 10-to-25-mile-per-hour winds all day long, Kelly felt right at home.

After rounds of 75 and 69 for an even-par 144, Kelly may be the only player in the field looking forward to an uncharacteristic cold snap.

"I prepare for it," said Kelly of how he deals with frigid conditions. "I've got my hand warmers. I know what gloves I'm going to wear. It's the same clothing I wear at home when I practice all the time."

And nothing stops the former all-city high school hockey player from practicing.

"I can't tell you how many times I've practiced when it's been below freezing," he said, warming up to the subject. "I mean that's a normal occurrence for me. A lot of times I'll have to hit from inside of a trailer with heaters and hit [the shots] out-side, but you always want to get out there on the grass."

Kelly said he would hit three balls off the turf outside and start to get frostbite, so he retreated to the sheltered, heated hitting bay he has at his home.

"I've definitely been used to it and prepared for it, but my body is getting a little bit old," said the 40-year-old.

"I love hearing guys gripe about things [like] oh, it's going to be cold, and it's going to rain."

Cold conditions coupled with winds bring another element into the equation at the Masters.

Players never feel like they're warm enough no matter how they're dressed. They also don't feel comfortable bundled up trying to play golf, let alone on a very difficult course such as Augusta National.

And finally, players sometimes get so chilly they make mental mistakes.

Kelly's hockey mentality may be why he is known as a tenacious player who is looking for a good finish in the 2007 Masters.

"I don't quit, period," he said. "Doesn't matter where I am; if I'm 10, 20 over, I could care less. I'm not going to quit. I'm going to try to make the next shot."

Kelly relishes the challenge.

"Tomorrow is going to be cold, no question," he said, smiling at the prospects.

"Yeah, lace 'em up, boys."

Jerry Kelly's bunker shot at the second green finished close to the hole, yielded a birdie, and produced a hearty smile from the golfer.

Hole No. 10 begins the challenging second nine at Augusta National.

Second-Round SCORING

Rounds	96
Below 70	3
Under par	12
Par	6
Over par	78
80 or over	13
Scoring average	75.628
Low score	68

Paul Casey,
Padraig Harrington

Second-Round Stat LEADERS

Driving distance
D. Love III, 300 yards

Driving accuracy
S. Verplank, L. Mize,
F. Funk, 13 of 14

Greens in regulation
J. Furyk, 16 of 18

Total putts
P. Harrington, 22

England's Luke Donald celebrated a good shot with his brother and caddie Christian during the round.

One of the favorite spectator spots during the week is around the water-guarded par-3 16th green.

Round Two LEADERS											Out									In	Rd2	Total
Pos.	Player	Par	1	2	3	4	5	6	7	8	9	36	10	11	12	13	14	15	16	17	18	In	Rd2	Total
			4	5	4	3	4	3	4	5	4	36	4	4	3	5	4	5	3	4	4	36	72	
T1	T. Clark		4	5	3	3	6	3	4	4	4	36	3	4	3	4	4	5	4	4	4	35	71	−2
T1	B. Wetterich		4	5	4	3	4	3	4	5	3	35	4	4	3	5	4	6	4	4	4	38	73	−2
3	V. Taylor		5	5	4	3	4	3	3	5	4	36	5	4	3	5	3	4	3	4	5	36	72	−1
T4	Z. Johnson		4	4	3	3	5	3	4	4	4	34	4	5	3	4	4	5	4	5	5	39	73	+0
T4	J. Kelly		4	4	4	3	3	3	3	4	4	32	4	4	3	5	4	5	3	4	5	37	69	+0
T4	J. Rose		5	5	4	3	4	3	4	5	4	37	5	4	3	5	4	5	3	4	5	38	75	+0
T4	V. Singh		4	4	4	3	4	2	5	4	4	34	4	5	3	5	3	5	4	4	4	37	71	+0

Appleby Tries to Make History

——— III ———

Although no Australian has ever won the Masters, Stuart Appleby shot 73 and took the 54-hole lead with a two-over-par 218 total. He hopes to break that streak but knows Tiger Woods and Justin Rose are just one stroke back.

The carefree blond hair cascades from under the brilliant white visor.

The Aussie, rugged and tan, looks like he should be on a surfboard hurtling toward Bondi Beach back home instead of walking the fairways at Augusta National Golf Club.

But today he's all business.

The 35-year-old Stuart Appleby is 15 years into his professional career. He owns eight PGA Tour wins and has won back at home, too. He was tied for fourth at the 2000 PGA and finished second in the 2002 British Open, losing in a playoff, but other than that, success in majors, especially here at the Masters, has proven elusive.

In 10 appearances, the 6-foot-1, 195-pound golfer has missed the cut five times and never finished better than a tie for 19th (2006).

"Certainly my past has never been flooded with appearances with someone like Tiger and many other major players," said Appleby.

After three days of this year's Masters,

Appleby can change his past in a dramatic way.

In spite of a triple-bogey seven at the next-to-last hole, which cut his lead from three strokes to one, Appleby shot 73 and totaled 218 strokes. He survived temperatures that didn't climb above the low 50s, wind chills in the 30s, and fickle gusts ranging from 10 to 25 miles per hour, which sent the scoring average to 77.35. It was the third-highest third round in Tournament history, topped only by 1952 (77.58) and 1956 (78.56).

Others didn't fare as well. Justin Rose (75) and Tiger Woods (72) fell a shot back of Appleby at 219, and Padraig Harrington (75), Zach Johnson (76), and Vaughn Taylor (77) were two back, at 220.

Bradley Dredge of Wales shot a 76 and stood in solo seventh at 221, and eight players, including Tim Clark (80), Phil Mickelson (73), and Retief Goosen (70), were at 222, six over par.

Goosen had the sole subpar score of the day, rebounding in a big way after just

Stuart Appleby scored a 7 on the 17th hole and saw a large lead dwindle.

Bogeys on the last three holes resulted in a 77, but still left Vaughn Taylor tied for fourth place.

making the cut, while Woods and Lee Westwood were the only players to match par in a round when 12 in the field shot 80 or higher.

That might have changed had Appleby not suffered a hiccup on the par-4 17th hole, hooking his tee shot into a bunker alongside the seventh green, hitting the lip and ricocheting into trees, and then finding a greenside bunker at 17 before three-putting for a seven.

Until that point, Appleby was in firm command as the only under-par player. His gaffe brought many players back into the hunt, including Woods, who finished earlier and saw the field come back to him in a large and haunting way.

"On 17 I hit a bad tee shot and really was trying to—from where I saw my lie, I thought, well, if I made a five, that will be pretty good," said Appleby, who is attempting to become the first Australian to win the Masters.

"And really, the whole day was a bit like that, you know, extracted pars sometimes, in really difficult situations where I thought maybe I need to realistically think about a bogey."

Tiger Woods shot 34–38—72 on Saturday.

After a third-round 79, Lucas Glover set his sights on a solid final-round finish with hopes of earning a 2008 invitation.

What They're Saying
(ROUND THREE)

There are too many rules in this game. They ought to let you take one ball, and if you lose it you come in.

—Past champion Fuzzy Zoeller, who'd prefer not to have to play in the cold and wind that made round three especially challenging

You know those tapes we have all seen of guys shooting 30 on the back nine? I don't think you're going to see that tape this year.

—Charles Howell III

I don't feel like there's a low enough number out there [Sunday] to catch everybody ahead of me. But now I can set my sights on finishing solid and earning a chance to drive back down Magnolia Lane next year.

—Lucas Glover assessing his Masters chances from six shots back

U.S. Open champion Geoff Ogilvy shot an 81 as most players struggled in very difficult third-round conditions.

Until then Appleby recorded three birdies, at Nos. 2, 3, and 4, all from inside 10 feet, in a first nine of 34. Eight pars on the second nine and the triple bogey left him with a 73, which jumped him from tied for eighth to the top of the leader board.

The endgame of his score left Appleby paired with Woods in the final grouping, a sobering fact for many, but not one the Aussie is worrying about.

Nor, he said, is Woods likely thinking about anything but his own game.

"He won't even know I'm there," said Appleby of his fellow competitor. "I'm sure I'll know he's there. He'll be the other guy."

The "other guy" is something else around these parts, someone who may be the greatest player the game has ever known when his career ends.

It has been an un-Tiger-like week for the Florida resident.

Like many, Woods has fought a loose driver for three days and for the second time in three rounds finished bogey-bogey.

How troubling was the finish?

"Very, very," said Woods. "Just got the wrong gust at the wrong time and that's the way it goes."

Although he finished well ahead of the leaders, he appeared to be much farther back than he ended up when his round concluded. By day's end, all that had changed.

His three-birdie, three-bogey round, he said, was better but not up to his liking entirely.

"It was a tough day with the wind gusts. That's just the way it is here. Hopefully, you get committed to hit the proper shot and get lucky at the same time with the wind."

Woods said that the wind, which was expected to be less prevalent in the final round than it was in the third round, could affect putting as well as tee-to-green play.

"If it blows like this, you don't know," he said.

"Putts from two and three feet you've got to play a little bit of wind. And that's trouble out here."

Woods knows his game hasn't been sharp. Numbers tell the tale.

He's hit only 52.4 percent of the fairways and 61.1 percent of the

Arms sent skyward, Texan J. J. Henry celebrated a chip-in birdie during his round.

Did You Know?
(ROUND THREE)

England's Lee Westwood has played three unusual Masters rounds. His scorecard has been dotted with ups and downs. In 54 holes, Westwood has made 20 pars, 14 birdies, 19 bogeys, and one triple bogey. And the third round was symptomatic of his week. He made six pars, six birdies, and six bogeys to shoot 72.

When Stuart Appleby finished at two-over-par 218 after 54 holes, it set a record for the highest third-round aggregate. Jack Nicklaus and Tommy Jacobs held the previous mark of even-par 216 in the 1966 Tournament.

There have been six Tournaments where there have been no scores in the 60s in the third round, including this year. Previous years include 1952, 1956, 1960, 1963, and 1966.

Through the first 70 Masters, an Australian has never won a Green Jacket. Australians have won the U.S. Open, the British Open, and the PGA Championship, but not the Masters . . . yet. Third-round leader Stuart Appleby can change that fact.

Despite five bogeys, Iowa native Zach Johnson shot a 76 and was tied for fourth place heading into the final round.

What They're Writing
(ROUND THREE)

Brett Quigley was one of the few combatants with a smile on his face Saturday at Augusta National.

And the Masters rookie shot 7-over-par 79 to fall into a tie for 51st entering the final round. But Quigley took solace in being able to fly home to Jupiter, FL., tonight to see wife Amy and daughter Lillian Sage Augusta, born Wednesday morning, just hours after he left in the middle of a practice round.

It seemed fitting his newest sponsor, an executive jet airline, will provide a 13-seat Gulfstream 4 for Quigley's party of nine.

Quigley still had the white hospital bracelet on his right wrist and pictures of Lillian in his yardage book. And he had mixed emotions Friday about making the cut on the 150 number.

"I knew I'd make the cut because I wanted to go home," said Quigley, who had 15 family and friends at his rental home watching the cut countdown. "I didn't watch the telecast, but I knew what was happening with all the screaming. It would have been a blessing if I missed [the cut], but I'm glad I'm here. I'm ready to go home and excited to go see Lillian and Amy."

—Bruce Berlet, Hartford Courant

Angel Cabrera signed his card, walked stiffly from the scorer's hut up the hill to the Augusta National golf club lawn and smiled. An unlikely reaction from the man who had just posted a 9-bogey 79 for the Saturday round of his favorite major championship: "How cold it was out there? A winter day in Scotland without the rain!"

Three of the toughest days in any recent-years Masters concluded with Australian Stuart Appleby going into final round play with a single stroke lead over favorite Tiger Woods and England's Justin Rose, Appleby giving up a large slice of the convincing lead he'd held most of the afternoon with a triple-bogey at the 17th.

As indication of the difficulty each and every player encountered when Woods completed his round in even-par 72 mid-afternoon he was six shots behind the leader, twelve players comfortably ahead of his 3-over par total.

After two hours of the self-inflicted mayhem on Augusta's back nine, the world number one ended up in the perfect position from which to vault into his fifth Green Jacket and add yet another record to his ever-growing list—highest winning score ever! That presently stands at 289, 1-over par, established in 1954 (Sam Snead) and repeated in 1956 (Jackie Burke).

Nobody survived unscathed during a cold day where bright sunlight belied the fact the centigrade temperature never rose higher than single digits, where a sharp chill wind constantly blustered and occasionally howled through the pines and azaleas. Disasters were so commonplace it was hard to keep track of each and every moment.

—David Mackintosh, Buenos Aires Herald

Forget the green jacket. How about a wool coat, scarf and mittens?

That was the necessary wardrobe Saturday at Augusta National, where spring turned to winter, scores soared and the 71st Masters had another in a long list of remarkable days.

For the first time since 1966, no player managed to break 70 during the third round as competitors retreated to depths never seen at this tournament.

Australia's Stuart Appleby emerged as the leader through 54 holes when getting to the warmth of the clubhouse was perhaps his greatest achievement.

—Bob Harig, St. Petersburg Times

By the time second-round co-leader Brett Wetterich trudged onto the 18th green Saturday, the sun had sunk below the pines, the temperature hovered near 40 degrees and only about 100 fans remained to applaud his day. It was a fitting, if sad, ending. Wetterich shot an 83 in Round 3. It was a disastrous day, even by Saturday's disastrous standards.

"Terrible," said Wetterich. "Terrible and frustrating."

If it makes him feel better, Wetterich's day was repeated, to varying degrees, all over the course. The average score of 77.35 was the highest third-round average in the last 25 years.

—Paul Daugherty, Cincinnati Enquirer

Patrons gather in large numbers around the 18th hole to watch players complete their rounds.

Phil Mickelson

(ROUND THREE)

This has been an unusual Tournament for golf's most celebrated lefty.

As thoroughly as Phil Mickelson prepared for his title defense, his play has been less than expected.

In 2004, he shot a nine-under-par 279 and birdied the last hole to win. Last year he scored a seven-under-par 281 and won by two strokes. In 2007 the two-time winner tussled with the cold, windy conditions and posted a one-over-par 73.

"This is as tough as I've seen," said Mickelson after a two-birdie, three-bogey round.

"It wasn't as hard as it could have been because they put water on the greens. [I don't] think it's impossible. I will try to gather a game plan tonight. It's tough to be aggressive at all with these conditions."

Mickelson just needs to look at his 2007 statistics to get an idea of where his troubles have been this year.

When he won in 2004 and 2006, the left-handed golfer hit 73.2 and 62.5 percent of his fairways and 73.6 and 69.4 percent of his greens in regulation, respectively.

His greens-in-regulation figures, a key element at Augusta National when coupled with Mickelson's deft putting touch, ranked first and fourth, respectively.

This year, Mickelson's driving accuracy ranks last (19 of 42 fairways) among those making the cut. He's hit about 46 percent of the fairways and greens in regulation daily. Mickelson ranks tied for 44th in greens hit.

Nonetheless, his six-over-par total of 222 left him only four shots behind Stuart Appleby's leading total.

So as the 36-year-old headed to the final round of the 2007 Masters, he remained optimistic about his chance to repeat.

"I don't feel like it's unrealistic," he said of a possible come-from-behind win that would earn a third Masters title and second in a row.

"I've seen people come from seven shots back. Obviously I needed to shoot under par [today] to really put myself in contention. I fought hard enough to where at least I have a chance. I have to figure out a way to make 14 pars and four birdies."

Mickelson said the four par-5s present birdie opportunities "but you're limited on any others, and fighting for pars is going to be very challenging."

Adding to his challenge is the fact that since 1990 the final pairing has produced the winner.

Mickelson knows that fact only too well.

"Historically, the winner has come from the final pairing," he said, knowing Woods and Appleby, the leader, are in that two-ball, "and that's because the wind dies down and you can shoot a good score."

"That will be different tomorrow. There's a good chance that a player, by going off earlier, could possibly take the title this year."

And that possibility is what Mickelson is counting on.

greens in regulation. He's made only nine birdies, six of them coming on the par 5s, and he's played the par 4s through three rounds in six over par.

Yet he's optimistic, as you would expect.

"I've got a shot at it," he said.

Plenty of others, perhaps everyone within five or six shots, can say the same. But it will take a sub-70 round to hang a Green Jacket in your locker at Augusta.

Given the conditions, there may not be a

Phil Mickelson played his way around Augusta National in 73 strokes, leaving him four behind the leaders after 54 holes.

round like that possible if a player is close enough to be in contention.

Rose, a 36-hole leader three years earlier, thinks steady golf could make him the first British Masters winner since Nick Faldo in 1996.

He's guarding against thinking too far ahead. There will be no prepared Masters speeches, because that is deadly.

"It's going to enter your mind the rest of today, tomorrow morning, if you're in there with a legitimate chance to win, but I think the key is when you're out there on the golf course, do you stay in the moment?" he admitted candidly.

"If you catch yourself getting ahead, which pretty much every player will do,

HOLE NO. 17

Par 4, 440 yards

Name: Nandina

The 17th hole requires a precise tee shot. The Eisenhower Tree stands sentinel in the left-center of the fairway, making placement critical. Knowing that, Stuart Appleby nearly shot himself out of the 54-hole lead at the 12th-hardest hole of the day. He hooked his tee shot into a bunker by the seventh green. He hit the lip with his second shot, which kicked the ball into the trees. His third found a greenside bunker. A splash out of the sand and three putts later, Appleby had a triple-bogey seven. It was the only blemish on the day that turned a three-shot lead to one. Appleby wasn't alone in his troubles. Contenders Tiger Woods, Justin Rose, and Vaughn Taylor all made bogeys there as well.

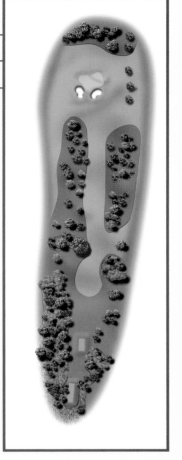

A triple bogey at the par-4 17th hole cut Stuart Appleby's lead to a single stroke heading into the final round.

Retief Goosen's 70 in cold, windy conditions was the only under-par score of the third round.

Australian Stuart Appleby shot a 73 and held a one-stroke lead.

In a reflective moment during the round, Vijay Singh and his caddie, Chad Reynolds, check their yardage.

it's just a matter of realizing it and bringing yourself back into the moment really."

Of all the contenders, Harrington, Taylor, and Johnson have remained largely in the background, as much by their quiet personalities as well as the distance they've remained from the top of the leader board. Close enough not to lose sight of the leaders but not close enough to draw scrutiny and, therefore, added pressure.

Harrington rebuffed any talk of doing something "special" for the final round.

"Let's talk about that after the Tournament," he said. "I have to go and do a job between now and the rest of the Tournament."

"You never know what's going to happen," said Taylor, who would like to follow Larry Mize's 1987 victory by an Augusta native.

"I always think of someone making a back-nine charge. As difficult as it is, it's tough to see that happening. Hopefully I can pull something special off tomorrow and see what happens on the back nine." ▮

Zach Johnson kept himself in the hunt for a Green Jacket.

Masters patrons greeted Tiger Woods warmly at the 16th green.

Golden Bell is the shortest par 3 on the course. But at 155 yards, the 12th hole has helped decide many a Masters outcome.

Tim Clark visited the bunkers four times in the third round and found himself four strokes behind Stuart Appleby's lead.

Round Three LEADERS			1	2	3	4	5	6	7	8	9	Out	10	11	12	13	14	15	16	17	18	In	Rd3	Total
Pos.	Player	Par	4	5	4	3	4	3	4	5	4	36	4	4	3	5	4	5	3	4	4	36	72	
1	S. Appleby		4	4	3	2	4	3	5	5	4	34	4	4	3	5	4	5	3	7	4	39	73	+2
T2	J. Rose		5	6	4	3	4	3	3	5	4	37	5	4	2	5	5	4	4	5	4	38	75	+3
T2	T. Woods		4	5	3	3	4	3	4	4	4	34	4	4	4	4	4	5	3	5	5	38	72	+3
T4	P. Harrington		5	5	3	4	5	3	4	5	4	38	4	4	4	4	4	7	3	3	4	37	75	+4
T4	Z. Johnson		4	5	4	3	5	3	4	5	5	38	4	5	4	5	4	4	4	4	4	38	76	+4
T4	V. Taylor		5	5	4	3	4	4	4	5	5	39	4	4	3	5	4	4	4	5	5	38	77	+4

Phil Mickelson's third-round 73 left him tied for eighth place heading to the final round.

Third-Round
SCORING

Rounds	60
Below 70	0
Under par	1
Par	2
Over par	57
80 or over	12
Scoring average	77.35
Low score	70
Retief Goosen	

Third-Round Stat
LEADERS

Driving distance
P. Mickelson, 290 yards

Driving accuracy
T. Clark, C. Stadler, 13 of 14

Greens in regulation
R. Goosen, 13 of 18

Total putts
L. Westwood, 23

Extricating himself from a bunker, Vaughn Taylor's 77 left him two shots out of the lead.

Johnson Calls Victory "Surreal"

---III---

Steady Zach Johnson, playing in only his third Masters Tournament, shot a sparkling 3-under-par 69 and totaled a record-tying high score of 289. It was good enough for a two-stroke victory over Tiger Woods, Retief Goosen, and Rory Sabbatini.

Day had long ago turned into night when Zach Johnson stood in the entryway of the stately white Clubhouse.

Long gone were his peers, off to Hilton Head, South Carolina, where a PGA Tour stop would take place, home, or parts unknown. Long gone, too, were the patrons who were most likely warming themselves from an unseasonably cool final round of the Masters.

As he looked down a darkened Magnolia Lane, the newest Masters champion couldn't help but think about the day and his future.

Hours earlier he had called his victory "surreal, very surreal."

Now the magnitude of it was beginning to sink in.

Now and forever he would walk in the history books of Masters lore.

Now and forever he would wear a Green Jacket every April when he returned to Augusta.

Now and forever he would walk through the same Clubhouse door, take about a dozen steps, and climb the narrow, twisting staircase to the second floor, turn left, and pass through the most difficult of doors to enter at Augusta National, the door to the Champions locker room—an oasis of peace and a place where history is alive and well.

Now and forever he would attend and listen to all the old Masters at the Champions dinner on Tuesday night tell tall tales of past Tournaments and one day probably get the chance to tell his own stories to champions younger than he.

How does this happen to a player in only his third Masters?

Only 11 past champions have won a Masters in three years or less, Gene Sarazen, Byron Nelson, Jimmy Demaret, and Tiger Woods among them.

How does a player with a previously undistinguished Masters record—a tie for 32nd and a missed cut—find his supreme game for the week and play himself into a 40 regular jacket?

Maybe it's his down-to-earth upbringing. Born in Iowa and raised in a middle-class

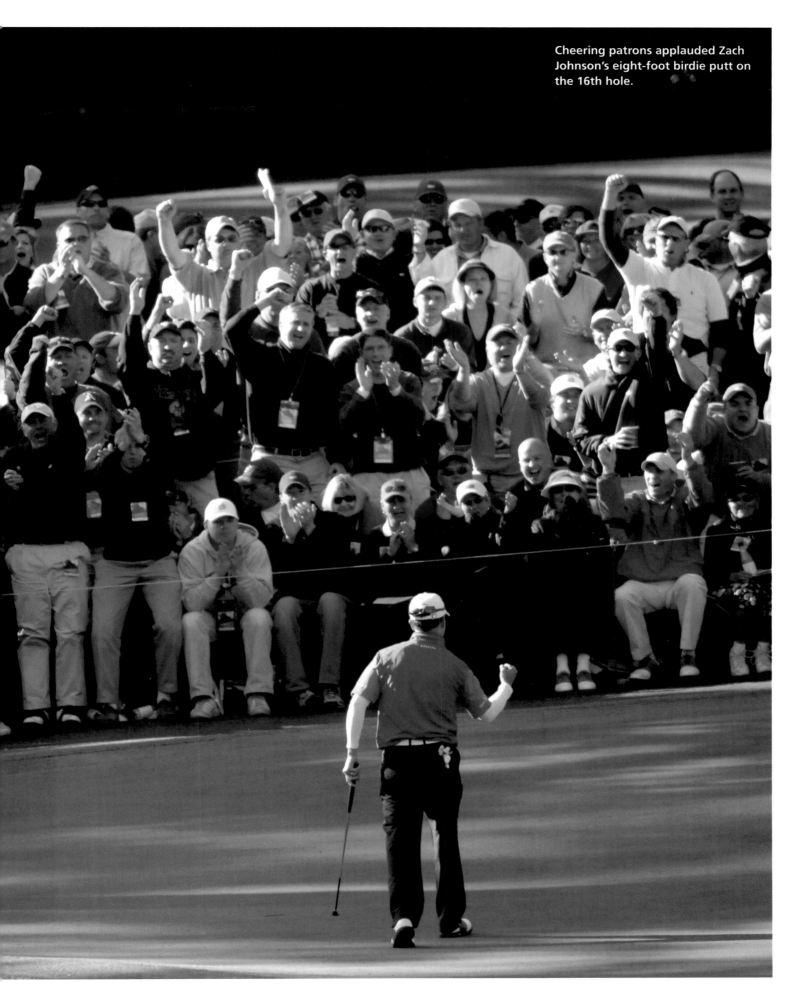

Cheering patrons applauded Zach Johnson's eight-foot birdie putt on the 16th hole.

Like many others, Vaughn Taylor was challenged by Augusta National's greens and made only two birdies in a round of 75.

family, Johnson is a humble man, a God-fearing man, and a family man, all things that can give you an inner peace in the most difficult of times; and certainly the final round of the Masters is one of the most difficult times in major championship golf.

Johnson's final-round 69 and one-over-par 289 aggregate, which tied the highest Masters winning total ever by Sam Snead (1954) and Jack Burke (1956), was two strokes better than Rory Sabbatini (69), Retief Goosen (69), and Woods (72), and three strokes better than Jerry Kelly (70) and Englishman Justin Rose (73).

Yet the numbers don't tell a fraction of the story.

On another unseasonably cool spring day, the second in a row, the raw nerves of the players in the final round were evident from the beginning.

Stuart Appleby's long bunker explosion was deft enough to earn a par at the difficult par-3 fourth hole.

What They're Saying

(ROUND FOUR)

I know that within myself that I had a chance to win today by the way I played. I know I can play this golf course. It is as comfortable as I have been all week and today was the most positive I have been on the golf course all week, and I had a chance today.

—*Englishman Ian Poulter after a two-under-par 70 and 296 total*

I think we all like a good challenge and Augusta National is a good challenge. You don't expect it to be easy-peasy; you have to earn it and then it is a lot more satisfactory when you do shoot your 70s or 69s.

—*Past champion Sandy Lyle on the difficulty of the Masters*

It's like you're going through a boxing match and you get knocked down each round. You just have to keep getting back up.

—*Sweden's Henrik Stenson on his tie for 17th place*

A picture-perfect blue sky is a backdrop for Tiger Woods's tee shot at the par-4 7th hole.

Surrounded by patrons, the final pairing of Stuart Appleby and Tiger Woods putt out on the ninth green.

While conditions were better than in the third round—and three rounds in the 60s and 13 subpar scores overall would prove it to be so—it didn't take long for hiccups to occur.

Third-round leader Stuart Appleby double-bogeyed the 455-yard, par-4 first hole and fell from the top. He eventually ended his title chances at the par-3 12th hole, finding the water fronting the green and making a second double bogey to finish with 75 and tie for seventh.

"I got off to a bad start with a double bogey on No. 1 and then another of No. 12," said Appleby. "It was a tough day."

Woods was in the lead after the third hole for the first time all week, fell out of the top spot with bogeys at Nos. 6 and 10, yet gave himself hope with a 24-foot eagle putt at the par-5 13th.

Despite hitting his second shot in the water at No. 15, Woods salvaged a par.

"I kept myself in the ball game," he said of the critical par at No. 15.

He said that he lost this Masters opportunity with bogey-bogey finishes during the first and third rounds.

"I threw this Tournament away on two days when I had two good rounds and I went bogey, bogey," he admitted. "So four bogeys in the last two holes basically cost me the Tournament."

With six players tied for or holding the lead midway through the round, Goosen seemed the most steady.

The South African made four birdies in his first-nine score of 32, but a three-putt bogey at No. 12 and the inability to make any birdies on the second nine spelled his fate.

Jerry Kelly scored a 34 on his last nine holes Sunday, equaling the low second nine on the final day.

Hole No. 11, a 505-yard par 4, was the fourth hardest hole on Sunday.

"I played very solid on the front nine, and on the back nine I played solid, too," Goosen said. "I just couldn't make a putt. I hit a couple of good shots coming in. Overall, I'm very happy. Obviously giving myself a chance again, but I would like to one year go a little bit further."

Sabbatini, also South African, can say the same thing.

He played the first nine with two birdies, and an eagle at No. 8, when he hit the green in two and sank a long putt from the back of the green, taking a bow afterward while the patrons cheered.

But his game faltered on the next hole, with a bogey. He would make two more birdies, at Nos. 13 and 18, but bogeys at No. 14, where his tee shot found the trees, and No. 16, where he missed the green long and failed to get up and down for par, cemented his doom.

While all this theater was unfolding around him, Johnson, who gained his experience on the minitours and the Nationwide

After Zach Johnson parred the 15th hole, he held a two-shot lead.

Tour before his regular Tour career began in 2004, kept his emotions in check.

Despite two bogeys and two birdies in the first five holes and a third birdie at the par-5 eighth via a chip-in, Johnson played the first nine in 35 and trailed first Sabbatini and then Goosen by one stroke.

As those around him stumbled, Johnson remained calm and collected.

Maybe it was because it was Easter Sunday and Johnson is a highly religious family man.

Rory Sabbatini ended the Tournament tied for second.

HOLE OF THE DAY
(ROUND FOUR)

HOLE NO. 16

Par 3; 170 yards

Name: Redbud

This hole has seen its share of drama over the years. Six-time champion Jack Nicklaus made a monstrous 40-foot birdie putt in 1975 en route to his fifth Masters. Tiger Woods holed an impossible-looking chip shot from behind the green to win in 2005. This year in the final round Redbud played a key role in Zach Johnson's victory and prevented pursuers from moving closer to the lead. Johnson's birdie putt was eight feet, and when it found the bottom of the cup it put him at even par and gave him a three-shot cushion. He hit a 6-iron. The hole played at 3.200 and gave up only seven birdies in the final round.

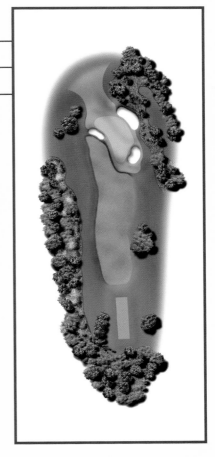

Did You Know?

(ROUND FOUR)

There were more eagles in the final round (10) than in the first three rounds combined (8).

—

When Tiger Woods finished in a second-place tie at three-over-par 291, including rounds of 73–74–72–72, it marked the first time in 11 Masters appearances as a professional that he failed to break par in any round. He had previously broken par 26 times, three times in all four rounds.

—

England's Justin Rose, who tied for fifth, had the wildest ride in the final round. He shot a 73, with six birdies; three double bogeys, including on the par-4 first hole; and one bogey. Champion Zach Johnson also had six birdies, but his winning 69 included only three bogeys.

—

There were 13 subpar final rounds. Shooting 69s—the low score of the day—were Zach Johnson, Rory Sabbatini, and Retief Goosen. There were only nine subpar rounds in the first round, 12 in the second, and one in the third.

—

The farthest back a Masters champion has ever come from is a tie for 25th: Bernhard Langer accomplished that in 1985. Champion Zach Johnson began the final round two strokes behind Stuart Appleby's lead and tied for fourth place.

Always the gentleman, Justin Rose tips his hat after tying for fifth place.

Maybe it was simply fate that gave him the inner peace on the second nine.

After three pars, Johnson birdied Nos. 13, 14, and 16, from 10, seven, and eight feet, respectively.

He took the lead for good with an 80-yard sand wedge shot at the par-5 13th, followed by a 10-foot birdie and a two-over-par total.

He stretched the lead to two at the 14th with his 7-iron second shot and a seven-foot birdie, and when his 6-iron stopped within eight feet of the 16th hole and he made a birdie, it likely sealed his victory.

With that final birdie Johnson had returned his score to even par, a rarity given the cold, windy conditions over the final 36 holes.

A bogey at No. 17, when his 7-iron missed the green short and left, cut his victory margin from three to two in the end. A key chip at No. 18 to save par ended the round.

Striking his irons superbly most of the week, Zach Johnson hit 44 of 72 greens in regulation en route to his victory.

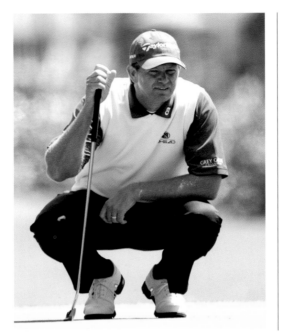

Retief Goosen scored a first-nine 32 on Sunday.

He knew his pre-Tournament preparation had been good, as had his state of mind.

But to win a major such as the Masters in only his third year on the PGA Tour was unexpected.

"I felt like my game was good coming into today," he said afterward. "I felt like I had a chance to really move up the board. I just feel very blessed and very honored."

This is a man who played on the Drake University golf team in Des Moines, Iowa, and wasn't even the best player, but became better each year leading up to the Masters.

This is a man who "didn't have any money" when he graduated and found financial backing from a host of friends to

Jerry Kelly's final-round 70 earned him a tie for fifth place and a trip back to the 2008 Masters.

Rory Sabbatini

(ROUND FOUR)

Rory Sabbatini considers himself a "type A" personality on the golf course.

He's a high-strung and aggressive individual.

But in golf that's not necessarily a catalyst for success. Sports psychologists will tell you that an even-keel attitude will get you farther in the game. Emotions, they tell you, need to be in check.

Sabbatini, 31, is learning that the hard way.

He's learned it by less-than-satisfactory results in majors, including the Masters.

In four previous trips to Augusta, Sabbatini has missed the cut three times, and he finished tied for 36th in 2006.

So the South African began the 2007 season with a new goal.

"My history in majors has been far from anything spectacular," he said. "One of my goals the past year has been to improve on my performance in the majors."

Sabbatini's tie for second was a good start.

He shot rounds of 73–76–73–69—291, three over par, and finished behind Zach Johnson's winning total of one-over-par 289.

And if Sabbatini needs any reinforcement that his plan to improve on his major finishes is working, he only needs to realize that he could have won the Masters with a little luck.

On a day when bright sun helped cut the edge on cool temperatures and light winds, Sabbatini was one of six players who either held the outright lead or shared it with Johnson.

For part of the final round Sabbatini held the solo lead at two over par when he sank a magnificent putt on the 570-yard, par-5 eighth hole for an eagle 3.

"I hit a pretty good drive and got up there far enough," he said. "I think I had about like 250, 255 yards left to the hole. I took a 2-iron and actually didn't feel like I hit it all that solid, but, you know, I hit it on the line I wanted to."

The shot finished at the back of the green, and the pin was on the front. Sabbatini's left-to-right swinging putt turned into the hole on one of the last rotations of his golf ball.

"I practiced that putt obviously a lot on Monday on the back of the green towards the front to get a sense of how it fed down toward the green, so I had a good idea of where I needed to put it in order to control the speed on the green."

Following that momentum changer, Sabbatini made three bogeys and two birdies on the second nine, including a 25-footer at the 18th hole to finish tied for second with Goosen and Woods.

"Maybe the plan for better patience in the majors is working," said Sabbatini.

"I just basically decided I need to play smarter, especially being more focused on where I placed the ball," he said of a key in any major, but particularly at Augusta National.

"Knowing when I can attack and when I need to be a little more cautious, and accept the fact that par is a good score and not trying to birdie every hole is important."

Putts fell with frequency for Rory Sabbatini, allowing him to finish in a three-way tie for second.

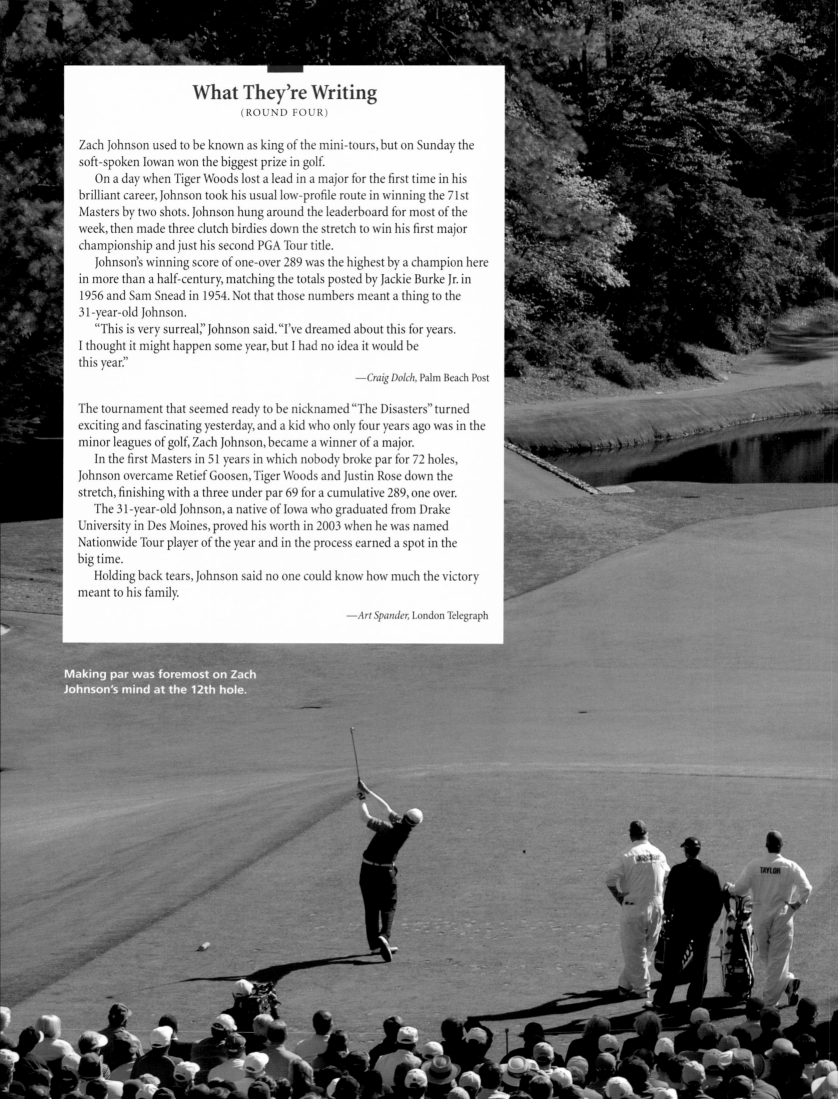

What They're Writing
(ROUND FOUR)

Zach Johnson used to be known as king of the mini-tours, but on Sunday the soft-spoken Iowan won the biggest prize in golf.

On a day when Tiger Woods lost a lead in a major for the first time in his brilliant career, Johnson took his usual low-profile route in winning the 71st Masters by two shots. Johnson hung around the leaderboard for most of the week, then made three clutch birdies down the stretch to win his first major championship and just his second PGA Tour title.

Johnson's winning score of one-over 289 was the highest by a champion here in more than a half-century, matching the totals posted by Jackie Burke Jr. in 1956 and Sam Snead in 1954. Not that those numbers meant a thing to the 31-year-old Johnson.

"This is very surreal," Johnson said. "I've dreamed about this for years. I thought it might happen some year, but I had no idea it would be this year."

—*Craig Dolch,* Palm Beach Post

The tournament that seemed ready to be nicknamed "The Disasters" turned exciting and fascinating yesterday, and a kid who only four years ago was in the minor leagues of golf, Zach Johnson, became a winner of a major.

In the first Masters in 51 years in which nobody broke par for 72 holes, Johnson overcame Retief Goosen, Tiger Woods and Justin Rose down the stretch, finishing with a three under par 69 for a cumulative 289, one over.

The 31-year-old Johnson, a native of Iowa who graduated from Drake University in Des Moines, proved his worth in 2003 when he was named Nationwide Tour player of the year and in the process earned a spot in the big time.

Holding back tears, Johnson said no one could know how much the victory meant to his family.

—*Art Spander,* London Telegraph

Making par was foremost on Zach Johnson's mind at the 12th hole.

Right from the start there was something in Justin Rose that encouraged the highest hopes. Not just in his talent but in his nature, his understanding of the vagaries and cruelties of life as well as golf.

This—we learned amid the dusk and the fireflies last night—was not an illusion. He didn't win the fabled green jacket, not quite, but he did earn something almost as valuable. He proved, beyond serious doubt, that he was rather more than one old and fading burst of youthful promise.

Before his challenge ended at the 17th he had shown that he had the game and the nerve to compete at the highest level. It was something on which to build, surely; something to say that he would be back with serious intent.

This wasn't the salvaging of a little bruised pride. This was the bravest run at the glory.

— *James Lawton*, Independent

The inspiring trip down Magnolia Lane is a little more than 350 venerable yards, making the journey through the 61 leafy giants the shortest drive at Augusta National.

Since 2001, Augusta National has bulked up, adding some 460 yards in a defiant attempt to counter the advances in technology and player performance. It's a development many believed all but eliminated the short- and medium-length hitter and narrowed the list of potential winners to a half dozen bombers.

But, as is the norm at Augusta, perception has been slow to jump on board with reality. The result—at least for the previous two dry, crusty years—was a Masters leaderboard that was a mosaic of the medium-lengthed as well as the mighty.

"Last year, so much was written about how long it was and how it would suit the longer player," said Tim Clark, who finished runner-up at Augusta in 2006 and 13th this year. "In the end, the length may have brought guys of my length back into the tournament."

Planning, precision and putting, not pounding, won the 71st Masters. Zach Johnson, one of the Tour's clutch putters who has never ranked better than 113th in driving distance, spent the days leading up to the Masters fine tuning his game at Frederica Golf Club on Sea Island, Ga., a Tom Fazio design with enough elevation and closely cropped chipping areas to pull off a serviceable Augusta National impersonation.

—*Rex Hoggard,* Golfweek

Shot of the Day
(ROUND FOUR)

By the time he reached the tee at the 450-yard, par-4 seventh hole, South African Retief Goosen found himself one stroke behind Tiger Woods for the early Masters lead. So when Goosen pulled his tee shot into the left trees, it looked like hard work was ahead. But he played a nearly blind, fearless shot, threading a wedge through an opening in the trees and over the top of other tall pines. The deftly executed shot landed just over the front bunker and stopped dead, five feet from the hole. He made a birdie and tied for the lead temporarily.

A sparkling final-round 69 wasn't enough for Retief Goosen to earn a Green Jacket.

support the early days of his career while he learned how to compete and win.

This is a man who won twice on the Nationwide Tour in 2003 and was named Player of the Year there, earning $494,882 and his PGA Tour card.

This is a man who earned a spot on the 2006 U.S. Ryder Cup Team and gained invaluable experience under the worldwide microscope that that event brings.

This is a man with his feet on the ground each and every day, even if his head is in the clouds after winning.

"I'm as normal as they come," said the 31-year-old.

"I love to play a game for a living. I love to play this game for what it is, golf. I appreciate it."

And now it appreciates you as the new Masters champion. ▐

With a pump of his fist, Zach Johnson celebrates his fifth birdie of the day, this time at the 14th hole.

With his round complete, Zach Johnson salutes patrons around the 18th green.

Padraig Harrington took his frustration out on a stubborn putter in the final round.

Squinting into the afternoon sun, Vaughn Taylor followed a drive that set up a birdie on the 15th hole.

Zach Johnson tied for second in driving accuracy and tied for fourth in greens in regulation; both played a key role in his win.

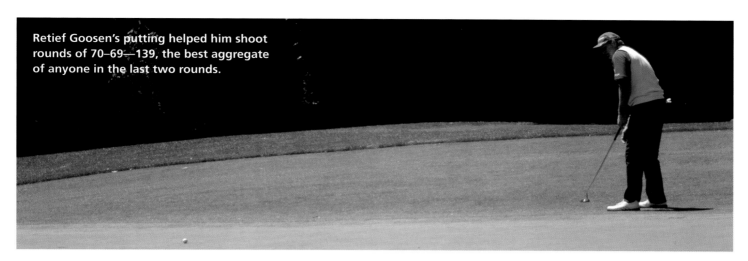

Retief Goosen's putting helped him shoot rounds of 70–69—139, the best aggregate of anyone in the last two rounds.

Zach Johnson, left, had good friend Vaughn Taylor as his fellow competitor during the final round.

Fourth-Round SCORING

Rounds	60
Below 70	3
Under par	13
Par	7
Over par	40
80 or over	5
Scoring average	74.331
Low score	69

Zach Johnson, Rory Sabbatini, Retief Goosen

Fourth-Round Stat LEADERS

Driving distance
G. Ogilvy, 299 yards

Driving accuracy
B. Quigley, 13 of 14

Greens in regulation
S. Cink, 16 of 18

Total putts
T. Herron, M. Weir, S. Ames, 24

Round Four LEADERS

Pos.	Player	Par	1	2	3	4	5	6	7	8	9	Out	10	11	12	13	14	15	16	17	18	In	Rd4	Total
			4	5	4	3	4	3	4	5	4	36	4	4	3	5	4	5	3	4	4	36	72	
1	Z. Johnson		5	4	3	3	5	3	4	4	4	35	4	4	3	4	3	5	2	5	4	34	69	+1
T2	R. Goosen		4	4	3	3	4	3	3	4	4	32	4	4	4	5	4	5	3	4	4	37	69	+3
T2	R. Sabbatini		4	4	3	3	4	3	4	3	5	33	4	4	3	4	5	5	4	4	3	36	69	+3
T2	T. Woods		5	4	4	3	4	4	4	5	4	37	5	4	3	3	4	5	3	4	4	35	72	+3
T5	J. Kelly		5	4	4	3	4	3	4	5	4	36	5	4	3	3	4	4	3	4	4	34	70	+4
T5	J. Rose		6	4	6	4	4	3	4	4	3	38	4	3	3	5	4	4	2	6	4	35	73	+4

Faith

▌▌▌

Through all the years of playing his way to golf's highest level, Zach Johnson never lost faith in his ability or his faith in God and family. That belief resulted in his first Masters title and a lifetime of memories.

His road to the Masters was often a winding and lonely one, relegated at times to the outposts of golf's netherworld.

But faith in himself and the Lord has led Zach Johnson to believe that better days were always ahead.

He believed that when he was at Regis High School in Cedar Rapids, Iowa, struggling to learn the game.

He believed that at Drake University in Des Moines, Iowa, when he wasn't the No. 1 golfer on his college team.

He believed that while driving the farm belt's back roads playing the Prairie Golf Tour in Iowa, Kansas, Nebraska, and Missouri, collecting sometimes minuscule checks but plenty of experience along the way.

And he believed that on the Nationwide Tour, where he was Player of the Year in 2003, and the PGA Tour, where he won the 2004 BellSouth Classic, his only victory prior to the Masters.

Faith has always been a big part of the new champion's life.

He is a devout Christian and a family man, a quiet soul who prefers to let his actions speak for him.

They spoke loud and clear at Augusta National Golf Club, because Johnson was well prepared for the first major of the year.

The 31-year-old, who now lives in Lake Mary, Florida, spent the week prior to the Masters with his sports psychologist, Dr. Morris Pickens, and his teacher, Mike Bender, at Sea Island, Georgia.

While Pickens worked on Johnson's mental preparation, Bender worked on the physical one.

During their lessons Bender made his pupil hit two shots and play the worse one, a game Ben Hogan called "worst ball," knowing handling bad shots effectively is key to scoring in the Masters.

He also knew that Johnson's lack of length on a 7,445-yard, par-72 layout would require that he have a sharp wedge game.

He was right on both accounts.

As is tradition, 2006 Masters winner Phil Mickelson helped Zach Johnson into his new Green Jacket.

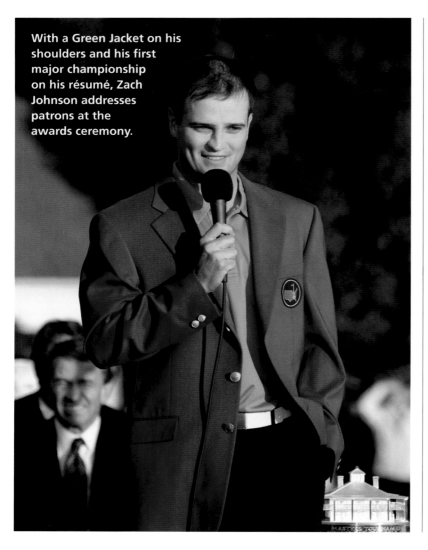

With a Green Jacket on his shoulders and his first major championship on his résumé, Zach Johnson addresses patrons at the awards ceremony.

Despite firm, fast conditions, Johnson's driving distance was statistically near the bottom of the field.

Everything else was superb.

A strategy of laying up on the four par 5s was smart. Unless his drives were long enough, Johnson knew he couldn't reach the long holes in two shots without a large risk.

By week's end, the newest champion hit 61.1 percent of the 72 greens in regulation, which ranked tied for fourth. He was tied for 10th in putting on surfaces that were made even more treacherous by the wind and cold. And he was tied for second in driving accuracy, hitting 80.36 percent of the fairways.

Add all that up and Johnson finished the week with 15 birdies and 16 bogeys. There were no crippling numbers.

The Iowa-born golfer was 11 under par on the par 5s, a testament to course management and patience.

It wasn't spectacular, but it was effective—and winning—golf.

Quietly, Johnson was supremely proud of his execution and his heritage.

"I'm Zach Johnson and I'm from Cedar Rapids, Iowa," he said to the worldwide media following his win.

"I'm a normal guy." ∎

Number of Attempts before Winning First Masters

First Year	
Horton Smith	1934—284
Gene Sarazen	1935—282
Fuzzy Zoeller	1979—280
Second Year	
Jimmy Demaret	1940—280
Herman Keiser	1946—282
Third Year	
Byron Nelson	1937—283
Ralph Guldahl	1939—279
Claude Harmon	1948—279
George Archer	1969—281
Bernhard Langer	1985—282
Tiger Woods	1997—270
Zach Johnson	2007—289

Zach Johnson and his caddie, Damon Green, were an unbeatable team.

Posing for pictures, Zach Johnson and Phil Mickelson are happy to be the most recent Masters champions.

Results & Statistics

——— III ———

Player	Position	Scores				Total	Money
Zach Johnson	1	71	73	76	69	289	$1,305,000
Low Professional: Gold Medal							
Sterling Silver Replica Masters Trophy							
Crystal Vase, Day's Low Score (69), Round 4							
Retief Goosen (South Africa)	T2	76	76	70	69	291	$541,333
Runner-up: Silver Medal							
Sterling Silver Salver							
Crystal Vase, Day's Low Score (70), Round 3							
Crystal Vase, Day's Low Score (69), Round 4							
Rory Sabbatini (South Africa)	T2	73	76	73	69	291	$541,333
Runner-up: Silver Medal							
Sterling Silver Salver							
Crystal Vase, Day's Low Score (69), Round 4							
Pair of Crystal Goblets, Eagle, Round 4, Hole 8							
Tiger Woods	T2	73	74	72	72	291	$541,333
Runner-up: Silver Medal							
Sterling Silver Salver							
Pair of Crystal Goblets, Eagle, Round 4, Hole 13							
Jerry Kelly	T5	75	69	78	70	292	$275,500
Pair of Crystal Goblets, Eagle, Round 4, Hole 13							
Justin Rose (England)	T5	69	75	75	73	292	$275,500
Crystal Vase, Day's Low Score (69), Round 1							
Stuart Appleby (Australia)	T7	75	70	73	75	293	$233,812
Padraig Harrington (Ireland)	T7	77	68	75	73	293	$233,812
Crystal Vase, Day's Low Score (68), Round 2							
Pair of Crystal Goblets, Eagle, Round 4, Hole 13							
David Toms	9	70	78	74	72	294	$210,250
Paul Casey (England)	T10	79	68	77	71	295	$181,250
Crystal Vase, Day's Low Score (68), Round 2							
Pair of Crystal Goblets, Eagle, Round 2, Hole 2							
Luke Donald (England)	T10	73	74	75	73	295	$181,250
Pair of Crystal Goblets, Eagle, Round 2, Hole 2							
Pair of Crystal Goblets, Eagle, Round 4, Hole 8							
Vaughn Taylor	T10	71	72	77	75	295	$181,250

Player	Position	Scores				Total	Money
Tim Clark (South Africa)	T13	71	71	80	74	296	$135,937
Jim Furyk	T13	75	71	76	74	296	$135,937
Ian Poulter (England)	T13	75	75	76	70	296	$135,937
Vijay Singh (Fiji)	T13	73	71	79	73	296	$135,937
Stewart Cink	T17	77	75	75	70	297	$108,750
Tom Pernice Jr.	T17	75	72	79	71	297	$108,750
Pair of Crystal Goblets, Eagle, Round 4, Hole 2							
Henrik Stenson (Sweden)	T17	72	76	77	72	297	$108,750
Pair of Crystal Goblets, Eagle, Round 3, Hole 13							
Mark Calcavecchia	T20	76	71	78	73	298	$84,462
Pair of Crystal Goblets, Eagle, Round 4, Hole 2							
Lucas Glover	T20	74	71	79	74	298	$84,462
Pair of Crystal Goblets, Eagle, Round 2, Hole 15							
John Rollins	T20	77	74	76	71	298	$84,462
Mike Weir (Canada)	T20	75	72	80	71	298	$84,462
Stephen Ames (Canada)	T24	76	74	77	72	299	$63,800
Pair of Crystal Goblets, Eagle, Round 4, Hole 13							
Phil Mickelson	T24	76	73	73	77	299	$63,800
Geoff Ogilvy (Australia)	T24	75	70	81	73	299	$63,800
Pair of Crystal Goblets, Eagle, Round 3, Hole 13							
K. J. Choi (Korea)	T27	75	75	74	76	300	$53,650
Davis Love III	T27	72	77	77	74	300	$53,650
Adam Scott (Australia)	T27	74	78	76	72	300	$53,650
Fred Couples	T30	76	76	78	71	301	$43,085
Charles Howell III	T30	75	77	75	74	301	$43,085
Robert Karlsson (Sweden)	T30	77	73	79	72	301	$43,085
Scott Verplank	T30	73	77	76	75	301	$43,085
Lee Westwood (England)	T30	79	73	72	77	301	$43,085
Dean Wilson	T30	75	72	76	78	301	$43,085

Brett Wetterich shared the 18- and 36-hole leads.

Player	Position	Scores				Total	Money
Yong-Eun Yang (Korea)	T30	75	74	78	74	301	$43,085
Angel Cabrera (Argentina)	T37	77	75	79	71	302	$31,900
J. J. Henry	T37	71	78	77	76	302	$31,900
Tim Herron	T37	72	75	83	72	302	$31,900
Rod Pampling (Australia)	T37	77	75	74	76	302	$31,900
Jeev Milkha Singh (India)	T37	72	75	76	79	302	$31,900
Brett Wetterich	T37	69	73	83	77	302	$31,900
Crystal Vase, Day's Low Score (69), Round 1							
Sandy Lyle (Scotland)	43	79	73	80	71	3003	$26,825
Bradley Dredge (Wales)	T44	75	70	76	83	304	$22,533
David Howell (England)	T44	70	75	82	77	304	$22,533
Pair of Crystal Goblets, Eagle, Round 1, Hole 15							
Miguel Angel Jimenez (Spain)	T44	79	73	76	76	304	$22,533
Shingo Katayama (Japan)	T44	79	72	80	73	304	$22,533
José Maria Olazabal (Spain)	T44	74	75	78	77	304	$22,533
Jeff Sluman	T49	76	75	79	75	305	$18,560
Craig Stadler	T49	74	73	79	79	305	$18,560
Brett Quigley	51	76	76	79	75	306	$17,835
Pair of Crystal Goblets, Eagle, Round 4, Hole 13							
Aaron Baddeley (Australia)	T52	79	72	76	80	307	$17,255
Carl Pettersson (Sweden)	T52	76	76	79	76	307	$17,255
Rich Beem	54	71	81	75	81	308	$16,820
Pair of Crystal Goblets, Eagle, Round 1, Hole 13							
Pair of Crystal Goblets, Eagle, Round 4, Hole 13							
Ben Crenshaw	T55	76	74	84	75	309	$16,530
Niclas Fasth (Sweden)	T55	77	75	77	80	309	$16,530
Trevor Immelman (South Africa)	T55	74	77	81	77	309	$16,530
Arron Oberholser	58	74	76	84	76	310	$16,240
Billy Mayfair	59	76	75	83	77	311	$16,095
Fuzzy Zoeller	60	74	78	79	82	313	$15,950
Michael Campbell (New Zealand)	–	76	77	–	–	153	$10,000
Chris DiMarco	–	75	78	–	–	153	$10,000
Colin Montgomerie (Scotland)	–	76	77	–	–	153	$10,000
Mark O'Meara	–	77	76	–	–	153	$10,000

Player	Position	Scores				Total	Money
Tom Watson	–	75	78	–	–	153	$10,000
Thomas Bjorn (Denmark)	–	77	77	–	–	154	$10,000
Bart Bryant	–	72	82	–	–	154	$10,000
Chad Campbell	–	77	77	–	–	154	$10,000
Darren Clarke (N. Ireland)	–	83	71	–	–	154	$10,000
Ernie Els (South Africa)	–	78	76	–	–	154	$10,000
Sergio Garcia (Spain)	–	76	78	–	–	154	$10,000
Todd Hamilton	–	74	80	–	–	154	$10,000
John Kelly	–	77	77	–	–	154	Amateur
Joe Durant	–	80	75	–	–	155	$10,000
Fred Funk	–	82	73	–	–	155	$10,000
Bernhard Langer (Germany)	–	78	77	–	–	155	$10,000
Ben Curtis	–	76	80	–	–	156	$10,000
Nick O'Hern (Australia)	–	76	80	–	–	156	$10,000
Richie Ramsay (Scotland)	–	76	80	–	–	156	Amateur
Steve Stricker	–	77	79	–	–	156	$10,000
Ben Crane	–	79	78	–	–	157	$10,000
Johan Edfors (Sweden)	–	78	79	–	–	157	$10,000
Raymond Floyd	–	77	80	–	–	157	$10,000
Kenneth Ferrie (England)	–	75	83	–	–	158	$10,000
Paul Goydos	–	79	79	–	–	158	$10,000
Troy Matteson	–	79	79	–	–	158	$10,000
Pair of Crystal Goblets, Eagle, Round 2, Hole 2							
Robert Allenby (Australia)	–	79	80	–	–	159	$10,000
Shaun Micheel	–	82	77	–	–	159	$10,000
Gary Player (South Africa)	–	83	77	–	–	160	$10,000
Larry Mize	–	83	78	–	–	161	$10,000
Julien Guerrier (France)	–	83	81	–	–	164	Amateur
Hideto Tanihara (Japan)	–	85	79	–	–	164	$10,000
Camilo Villegas (Colombia)	–	80	85	–	–	165	$10,000
Casey Watabu	–	87	78	–	–	165	Amateur
Dave Womack	–	84	81	–	–	165	Amateur
Seve Ballesteros (Spain)	–	86	80	–	–	166	$10,000
Ian Woosnam (Wales)	Withdrew						$10,000

TOTAL $7,418,464

Zach Johnson successfully stuck to a game plan of laying up on par 5s.

Rounds	312
Below 70	8
Below par	35
Par	20
Over par	257
80 or over	42
Scoring average	75.883
Low score	68

Paul Casey, Padraig Harrington

Final Stat
LEADERS

Driving distance
P. Mickelson, 292.63 yards

Driving accuracy
T. Clark, 47 of 56

Greens in regulation
J. Furyk, 47 of 72

Total putts
P. Harrington, 107

Jim Furyk led the 2007 field in greens in regulation.

FINAL COURSE STATISTICS

Four-time winner Arnold Palmer acknowledges a warm welcome as the Honorary Starter for the 2007 Masters Tournament.

Hole	Yards	Par	Average	Rank*	Eagles	Birdies	Pars	Bogeys	Double Bogeys	Others
1	455	4	4.474	2	0	13	162	117	17	3
2	575	5	4.776	17	5	101	169	34	2	1
3	350	4	4.138	13	0	38	207	54	12	1
4	240	3	3.417	4	0	11	176	111	12	2
5	455	4	4.314	8	0	22	187	88	13	2
6	180	3	3.189	12	0	30	198	79	5	0
7	450	4	4.295	10	0	31	176	88	16	1
8	570	5	4.766	18	2	103	175	30	2	0
9	460	4	4.138	14	0	27	218	65	1	1
Out	3735	36	37.507		7	376	1668	666	80	11
10	495	4	4.375	6	0	21	174	99	15	3
11	505	4	4.510	1	0	15	154	117	22	4
12	155	3	3.401	5	0	27	177	72	30	6
13	510	5	4.846	16	9	89	167	38	6	3
14	440	4	4.321	7	0	31	161	109	11	0
15	530	5	4.981	15	2	81	170	47	6	6
16	170	3	3.304	9	0	21	183	101	6	1
17	440	4	4.215	11	0	33	185	89	4	1
18	465	4	4.423	3	0	26	147	124	12	3
In	3710	36	38.376		11	344	1518	796	112	27
Total	7445	72	75.883		18	720	3186	1462	192	38

*Holes ranked from 1 (most difficult) to 18 (least difficult).

All-Time Scoring Records

Low First Nine
30, Johnny Miller, third round, 1975
30, Greg Norman, fourth round, 1988
30, K. J. Choi, second round, 2004

Low Second Nine
29, Mark Calcavecchia, fourth round, 1992
29, David Toms, fourth round, 1998

Low 18
63 (33–30), Nick Price, third round, 1986
63 (33–30), Greg Norman, first round, 1996

Low First Round
63 (33–30), Greg Norman, 1996

Low Second Round
64 (31–33), Miller Barber, 1979
64 (33–31), Jay Haas, 1995

Low Third Round
63 (33–30), Nick Price, 1986

Low Fourth Round
64 (34–30), Maurice Bembridge, 1974
64 (32–32), Hale Irwin, 1975
64 (34–30), Gary Player, 1978
64 (30–34), Greg Norman, 1988
64 (35–29), David Toms, 1998

Low First 36 Holes
131 (65–66), Raymond Floyd, 1976

Low Middle 36 Holes
131 (66–65), Tiger Woods, 1997, 2005

Low Last 36 Holes
131 (65–66), Johnny Miller, 1975

Low First 54 Holes
201 (65–66–70), Raymond Floyd, 1976
201 (70–66–65), Tiger Woods, 1997

Low Last 54 Holes
200 (66–65–69), Tiger Woods, 1997

Low 72 Holes
270 (70–66–65–69), Tiger Woods, 1997

Highest Winning Score
289, Sam Snead, 1954
289, Jack Burke, 1956
289, Zach Johnson, 2007

Low 18-Hole Score by a First-Year Player
64 (32–32), Lloyd Mangrum, first round, 1940
64 (31–33), Mike Donald, first round, 1990
64 (35–29), David Toms, fourth round, 1998

Low 72 Holes by a First-Year Player
278 (71–66–74–67), Toshi Izawa, 2001

Low 18 by an Amateur
66 (32–34), Ken Venturi, first round, 1956

Low 72 Holes by an Amateur
281 (72–71–69–69), Charles R. Coe, 1961

SCORING SUMMARY

	Below 70	Under Par	Par	Over Par	80 & Over	Course Average	Round Leader	Low Round	Zach Johnson
Round 1	2	9	5	82	12	76.189	Justin Rose (69) Brett Wetterich (69)	Justin Rose (69) Brett Wetterich (69)	T5
Round 2	3	12	6	78	13	75.628	Tim Clark (142) Brett Wetterich (142)	Padraig Harrington (68) Paul Casey (68)	T4
Round 3	0	1	2	57	12	77.352	Stuart Appleby (218)	Retief Goosen (70)	T4
Round 4	3	13	7	40	5	74.331	Zach Johnson (289)	Zach Johnson (69) Rory Sabbatini (69) Retief Goosen (69)	1
All Rounds	8	35	20	257	42	75.883			

Past Champions

'06	Phil Mickelson	281		'69	George Archer	281
'05	Tiger Woods	276		'68	Bob Goalby	277
'04	Phil Mickelson	279		'67	Gay Brewer	280
'03	Mike Weir	281		'66	Jack Nicklaus	288
'02	Tiger Woods	276		'65	Jack Nicklaus	271
'01	Tiger Woods	272		'64	Arnold Palmer	276
'00	Vijay Singh	278		'63	Jack Nicklaus	286
'99	Jose Maria Olazabal	280		'62	Arnold Palmer	280
'98	Mark O'Meara	279		'61	Gary Player	280
'97	Tiger Woods	270		'60	Arnold Palmer	282
'96	Nick Faldo	276		'59	Art Wall	284
'95	Ben Crenshaw	274		'58	Arnold Palmer	284
'94	Jose Maria Olazabal	279		'57	Doug Ford	283
'93	Bernhard Langer	277		'56	Jack Burke	289
'92	Fred Couples	275		'55	Cary Middlecoff	279
'91	Ian Woosnam	277		'54	Sam Snead	289
'90	Nick Faldo	278		'53	Ben Hogan	274
'89	Nick Faldo	283		'52	Sam Snead	286
'88	Sandy Lyle	281		'51	Ben Hogan	280
'87	Larry Mize	285		'50	Jimmy Demaret	283
'86	Jack Nicklaus	279		'49	Sam Snead	282
'85	Bernhard Langer	282		'48	Claude Harmon	279
'84	Ben Crenshaw	277		'47	Jimmy Demaret	281
'83	Seve Ballesteros	280		'46	Herman Keiser	282
'82	Craig Stadler	284		'45	No tournament, WWII	
'81	Tom Watson	280		'44	No tournament, WWII	
'80	Seve Ballesteros	275		'43	No tournament, WWII	
'79	Fuzzy Zoeller	280		'42	Byron Nelson	280
'78	Gary Player	277		'41	Craig Wood	280
'77	Tom Watson	276		'40	Jimmy Demaret	280
'76	Raymond Floyd	271		'39	Ralph Guldahl	279
'75	Jack Nicklaus	276		'38	Henry Picard	285
'74	Gary Player	278		'37	Byron Nelson	283
'73	Tommy Aaron	283		'36	Horton Smith	285
'72	Jack Nicklaus	286		'35	Gene Sarazen	282
'71	Charles Coody	279		'34	Horton Smith	284
'70	Billy Casper	279				

Camilo Villegas, right, with veteran David Toms, was one of 18 first-time participants.

All-Time Masters Participants

Aaron, Tommy	1959–2005
Adams, John	1994–1994
Adams, Sam	1974–1974
Adams, Ted	1939–1939
Albert, Don	1954–1954
Alexander, Keith	1961–1961
Alexander, Skip	1948–1954
Alexander, Stewart M.	1987–1988
Allem, Fulton	1992–1994
Allen, Donald C.	1965–1967
Allenby, Robert	1997–2007
Allin, Bud	1973–1977
Alliss, Peter	1966–1967
Ames, Stephen	2005–2007
Andrade, Billy	1987–2002
Andrews, Gene	1958–1962
Angelini, Alfonso	1964–1964
Aoki, Isao	1974–1988
Appleby, Stuart	1997–2007
Archer, George	1967–1992
Arda, Ben	1962–1962
Armour III, Tommy	1990–1990
Armour, Tommy	1935–1942
Armstrong, Wally	1978–1979
Austin, Woody	1996–1996
Azinger, Paul	1987–2002
Baddeley, Aaron	2000–2007
Baiocchi, Hugh	1974–1976
Baird, Briny	2004–2004
Baird, Butch	1977–1977
Baker, Peter	1994–1994
Baker-Finch, Ian	1985–1996
Bakst, Ken	1998–1998
Balding, Al	1956–1968
Ball, Errie	1934–1957
Ballenger, Douglas S.	1973–1973
Ballesteros, Seve	1977–2007
Bannerman, Harry	1972–1972
Barbarossa, Robert	1969–1969
Barber, Jerry	1953–1967
Barber, Miller	1968–1980
Barnes Jr., Thomas W.	1966–1966
Barnes, Brian	1972–1973
Barnes, Ricky	2003–2003
Barnes, Thomas	1950–1950
Barr, Dave	1982–1988
Barron, Herman	1934–1950
Bassler, Charles	1952–1952
Baxter Jr., Rex	1955–1964
Bayer, George	1958–1966
Bean, Andy	1977–1990
Beard, Frank	1965–1976
Beck, Chip	1983–1995
Beem, Rich	2003–2007
Begay III, Notah	2000–2001
Belfore, Joe	1939–1939
Bell, Art	1948–1949
Beman, Deane R.	1959–1973
Bembridge, Maurice	1970–1976
Bendall Jr., Richard A	1972–1972
Benepe, Jim	1989–1991
Berganio Jr., David	1992–1997
Bernardini, Roberto	1969–1970
Bertolino, Enrique	1940–1940
Besselink, Al	1951–1955
Bies, Don	1968–1976
Billows, Ray	1939–1940
Bishop, Stanley	1952–1955
Bisplinghoff, Don	1956–1956
Bjorn, Thomas	1999–2007
Black, Ronnie	1984–1985
Blackburn, Woody	1977–1985
Blackmar, Phil	1986–1998
Bladon, Warren	1997–1997
Blair, David A.	1962–1963
Blake, Jay Don	1991–1993
Blancas Jr., Homero	1963–1975
Blum, Arnold	1952–1958
Bohmann, John	1969–1970
Bohn, Jason	2006–2006
Bolt, Tommy	1952–1972
Bonallack, Michael F.	1966–1970
Booe, William	1956–1956
Boros, Guy	1997–1997
Boros, Julius	1950–1974
Boynton, Frank	1969–1969
Bradley, Michael	1997–1998
Brannan, Michael A.	1978–1978
Brewer, Gay	1962–2001
Britton, Bill	1990–1991
Brooks, Mark	1989–2002
Brosch, Al	1937–1953
Brown, Billy Ray	1991–1998
Brown, Ken	1988–1988
Browne, Olin	1998–2006
Brownlee, Phillip	1961–1961
Bryant, Bart	2006–2007
Bryant, Brad	1995–1996
Bulla, Johnny	1940–1957
Burke Jr., Jack	1950–1974
Burke, Billy	1934–1961
Burkemo, Walter	1952–1964
Burns III, George	1975–1987
Burroughs, Clark D.	1984–1984
Butler, Peter J.	1964–1970
Byman, Bob	1979–1979
Byrd, Jonathan	2003–2004
Byrd, Sam	1940–1948
Byrum, Curt	1990–1990
Byrum, Tom	1990–2003
Cabrera, Angel	2000–2007
Calcavecchia, Mark	1987–2007
Caldwell, Rex	1980–1985
Campbell, Albert	1936–1936
Campbell, Chad	2003–2007
Campbell, Joe E.	1956–1958
Campbell, Michael	1996–2007
Campbell, William C.	1950–1976
Carmichael, Samuel H.	1962–1962
Carnevale, Mark	1993–1993
Carr, Joseph B.	1967–1969
Casey, Paul	2004–2007
Casper, Billy	1957–2001
Castator, Bruce	1959–1959
Cejka, Alexander	1996–2004
Cerda, Antonio	1961–1964
Cerrudo, Ronald J.	1966–1967
Chalmers, Greg	2001–2001
Chamblee, Brandel	1999–1999
Champ, Frank	1953–1953
Chapman, Richard D.	1939–1962
Charles, Robert J.	1958–1975
Chen, Tze-Chung	1986–1989
Chen, Tze-Ming	1986–1986
Cherry, Don	1953–1962
Chin, Chick	1936–1936
Ching-Po, Chen	1963–1968
Choi, K. J.	2003–2007
Cink, Stewart	1997–2007
Ciuci, Henry	1934–1935
Claar, Brian	1990–1990
Clampett, Bobby	1979–1983
Clark, Clarence	1935–1937
Clark, Clive	1968–1968
Clark, Fairley	1934–1934
Clark, Howard	1987–1987
Clark, Jimmy	1954–1954
Clark, Tim	1998–2007
Clarke, Darren	1998–2007
Clarke, Douglas B.	1980–1980
Clearwater, Keith	1988–1993
Clements, Lennie	1984–1988
Coceres, Jose	2001–2002
Cochran, Robert	1946–1962
Cochran, Russ	1992–1994
Coe, Charles R.	1949–1971
Colbert, Jim	1972–1984
Cole, Bobby	1967–1978
Coles, Neil C.	1966–1966
Collins, Bill	1961–1965
Coltart, Bruce	1941–1941
Combs, Michael S.	1991–1991
Congdon, Charles	1947–1947
Conner, Frank	1982–1982
Conrad, Joe	1955–1957
Coody, Charles	1963–2006
Cook, John	1979–2003
Cooper, Harry	1934–1942
Cooper, Pete	1949–1957
Cotton, Henry	1948–1957
Couples, Fred	1983–2007
Courville Jr., Jerry	1996–1996
Cowan, Gary	1962–1973
Cox, Wiffy	1934–1938
Crampton, Bruce	1957–1976
Crane, Ben	2006–2007
Crawford, Richard	1960–1960
Creavy, Tom	1934–1934
Crenshaw, Ben	1972–2007
Crosby, Nathaniel P.	1982–1984
Cruickshank, Bobby	1934–1942
Cudd, Bruce	1954–1957
Culligan III, Thomas J.	1972–1972
Cupit, Buster	1959–1959
Cupit, Jacky	1962–1968
Curl, Rod	1975–1976
Curry, David H.	1987–1988
Curtis, Ben	2004–2007
Dahlbender Jr., Gene	1949–1949
Daly, John	1992–2006
Davies, Richard D.	1963–1966
Davis, Brian	2004–2004
Davis, Rodger	1988–1992
Dawson, George	1940–1941
Dawson, John W.	1934–1952
Day, Glen	1999–2000
De Bendern, John	1949–1953
De Lamaze, Henri	1958–1958
De Lozier, Henri	1974–1976
De Vicenzo, Roberto	1950–1975
De Wit, Gerry	1962–1964
Deluca, Fidel	1962–1962
Demaret, Jimmy	1939–1967
Dennis, Clark	1995–1995
Desjardins, Paul	1963–1963
Devlin, Bruce	1962–1983
Dickerson, Ben	2002–2002
Dickinson Jr., Gardner	1954–1974
Dickson, Bob	1966–1974
Diegel, Leo	1934–1935
Diehl, Terry	1975–1978
Dill, Terry	1965–1967
DiMarco, Chris	2001–2007
Dodd, Stephen C.	1990–1990
Dodds, Trevor	1999–1999
Dodson, Leonard	1937–1941
Doering Jr., Art	1940–1941
Donald, Luke	2005–2007
Donald, Mike	1990–1991
Doser, Clarence	1953–1954
Dougherty, Dillon	2006–2006
Dougherty, Ed	1996–1996
Douglas, Dave	1950–1962
Douglass, Dale	1969–1971
Dow, Willie	1934–1934
Dredge, Bradley	2007–2007
Driscoll, James	2001–2001
Drury, Chip	1986–1986
Dudley, Ed	1934–1950
Dundas, Stephen	1993–1993
Dunlap Jr., George T.	1934–1934
Durant, Joe	1999–2007
Dutra, Mortie	1934–1935
Dutra, Olin	1935–1953
Duval, David	1996–2006
Eastwood, Bob	1984–1988
Eaton III, Austin	2005–2005
Edfors, Johan	2007–2007
Edwards, Danny	1977–1986
Edwards, David	1984–1996
Egan, Chandler	1935–1935
Eger, David	1989–1989
Eichelberger, Dave	1965–1982
Elder, Lee	1975–1981
Eldred, Vincent	1936–1936
Elkington, Steve	1991–2003
Ellis Jr., Wes	1957–1968
Ellis, Danny	1994–1994
Els, Ernie	1994–2007
Emery, Walter	1934–1934
Espinosa, Abe	1934–1935
Espinosa, Al	1934–1937
Estes, Bob	1994–2004
Estrada, Juan Antonio	1962–1964
Evans Jr., Charles	1940–1960
Evans, Duncan	1981–1981
Evans, Max	1955–1955
Fairfield, Don	1956–1964
Faldo, Nick	1979–2006
Farquhar, John	1961–1972
Farrell, John J.	1934–1956
Fasth, Niclas	2002–2007
Faxon, Brad	1992–2004
Fazio, George	1947–1954
Feherty, David	1992–1992
Fehr, Rick	1983–1995
Fergus, Keith	1976–1984
Ferrell, William E.	1965–1965
Ferrie, Kenneth	2007–2007
Ferrier, Jim	1940–1965
Fetchick, Mike	1957–1964
Fezler, Forrest	1975–1975
Finsterwald, Dow	1951–1967
Fiori, Ed	1980–1997
Fischesser, Douglas H.	1978–1980
Fitzsimons, Pat	1975–1976
Flanagan, Nick	2004–2004
Fleck, Jack	1956–1965
Fleckman, Marty	1969–1969
Fleisher, Bruce	1969–1992
Flesch, Steve	2001–2005
Fletcher, Pat	1955–1955
Floyd, Raymond	1965–2007
Fondren, W. D.	1934–1934
Fontanini, Sargio M.	1957–1957
Foote, Dick	1959–1959
Ford, Doug	1952–2000
Ford, Stephen J.	1988–1988
Forsbrand, Anders	1993–1994
Forsman, Dan	1986–1997
Foster, Rodney	1966–1966
Fought III, John A.	1977–1984
Foulis, Jim	1934–1947
Francis, Francis	1937–1937
Francis, Gene	1962–1962
Franco, Carlos	1999–2005
French, Emmet	1934–1934
Frisina, James	1952–1952
Frost, David	1987–1998
Fuhrer III, Frank B.	1982–1982
Fulke, Pierre	2001–2001
Funk, Fred	1993–2007
Funseth, Rod	1966–1979
Furgol, Ed	1947–1965
Furgol, Marty	1951–1959
Furyk, Jim	1996–2007
Gabrielsen, James R.	1963–1972
Gafford, Ray	1951–1952
Gallacher, Bernard	1970–1970
Gallagher Jr., Jim	1991–1996
Gamez, Robert	1990–1991
Garaialde, Jean	1964–1966
Garcia, Sergio	1999–2007
Gardner, Buddy	1986–1986
Gardner, Robert W.	1961–1965
Garrido, Antonio	1978–1978
Garrido, Ignacio	1998–1998
Geiberger, Al	1962–1980
Geiberger, Brent	2000–2000
Ghezzi, Victor	1934–1962
Gianferante, Jerry	1942–1942
Gibson, Andy	1941–1941
Gibson, Leland	1946–1955
Gilbert, Gibby	1971–1981
Gilder, Bob	1976–1993
Giles III, Marvin M.	1968–1977
Gilford, David	1995–1996
Glasson, Bill	1986–1999
Gleichmann, Ted	1957–1957
Glover, Lucas	2006–2007
Glover, Randy	1966–1966
Goalby, Bob	1960–1986
Goetz, Robert	1959–1959
Goggin, Willie	1935–1942
Golden, John	1934–1935
Goldman, David	1960–1960
Goldstrand, Joel	1971–1971
Gonzalez Diniz, Priscilo	1976–1976
Gonzalez Jr., José Maria	1962–1962
Gonzalez, Ernie	1987–1987
Gonzalez, Mario	1960–1962
Goodloe Jr., William L.	1951–1955
Goodman, Johnny	1936–1936
Goosen, Retief	1998–2007
Gossett, David	2000–2000
Gove, Michael S.	1980–1980
Goydos, Paul	1996–2007
Grace, John P.	1975–1976
Grady, Wayne	1990–1995
Graham, David	1971–1987
Graham, Lou	1969–1980
Grant, James A.	1966–1967
Gray, A. Downing	1963–1974
Green, Danny	1990–2000
Green, Hubert	1969–1990
Green, Ken	1986–1997
Greene, Charles H.	1966–1974
Gregson, Malcolm	1968–1968
Greiner, Otto	1949–1949
Groh, Gary	1975–1975
Guardiola, Richard	1964–1964
Guerrier, Julien	2007–2007
Guldahl, Ralph	1937–1973
Gump, Scott	1988–2000
Haas Jr., Fred	1935–1957
Haas, Hunter	2000–2000
Haas, Jay	1976–2005
Haas, Jerry L.	1985–1985
Haeggman, Joakim	2005–2005
Hagawa, Yutaka	1982–1983
Hagen, Walter	1934–1941
Hager, Joe	1981–1981
Haliburton, Thomas B.	1962–1962
Hall, C. W.	1934–1934
Hallberg, Gary	1978–1993
Halldorson, Dan	1981–1981
Hallet, James O.	1983–1983
Hamer, George	1947–1948
Hamilton, Bob	1946–1957
Hamilton, Robert	2002–2002
Hamilton, Todd	2004–2007
Hamman, Leland	1935–1935
Hammond, Donnie	1986–1991
Hancock, Phil	1981–1981
Harbert, Melvin	1939–1964
Hardin, Christian	1989–1989
Harmon, Claude	1946–1969
Harney, Paul	1959–1974
Harper, Chandler	1942–1962
Harrington, Padraig	2000–2007
Harris Jr., Labron	1963–1972
Harris, Bob	1956–1961
Harris, John	1994–1994
Harrison, Charles W.	1960–1973
Harrison, E. J.	1940–1968
Hart, Dudley	1994–2001
Hatalsky, Morris	1982–1991
Hawkins, Fred	1952–1962
Hayes, Dale	1975–1977
Hayes, J. P.	1999–1999
Hayes, Mark	1977–1984
Heafner, C. Vance	1978–1978
Heafner, Clayton	1940–1953
Heard, Jerry	1971–1979
Hebert, Jay	1954–1968
Hebert, Lionel	1956–1970
Heinen, Mike	1995–1995
Henke, Nolan	1991–1994
Henning, Harold R.	1960–1971
Henninger, Brian	1995–1996
Henry, George	1966–1970
Henry, J. J.	2007–2007
Hensby, Mark	2005–2006
Herron, Tim	1996–2007
Higashi, Satoshi	1996–1996
Hill, Dave	1968–1979
Hill, Mike	1973–1978
Hill, Ray	1950–1950
Hines, Jimmy	1934–1946
Hinkle, Lon	1979–1982
Hinson, Larry	1970–1972
Hiskey, Babe	1973–1974
Hitchcock, James	1966–1966
Hjertstedt, Gabriel	1998–2000
Hobby, Timothy L.	1990–1990
Hoch, Scott	1979–2003
Hoey, Michael	2002–2002
Hoffer, William A.	1984–1984
Hogan, Ben	1938–1967
Hogarth, Tim	1997–1997
Holguin, Tony	1949–1951
Holscher, Bud	1954–1956
Holt, William	1940–1940
Holtgrieve, James M.	1980–1984
Homer, Trevor	1973–1974
Hopkins Jr., Edwin	1956–1956
Hopkins, John Mark	1965–1966
Horn, Rodney	1966–1966
Horne, Stan	1938–1939
Horton, Tommy	1968–1977
Horvath, Rudy	1955–1955
Houghton, Al	1934–1934
Howe III, Ralph	1989–1989
Howell III, Charles	2002–2007
Howell, Billy	1934–1934
Howell, David	2005–2007
Hsieh, Min-Nan	1983–1983
Hsieh, Yung-Yo	1970–1972
Huggett, Brian	1969–1969
Hughes, Bradley	1998–1998
Hulbert, Mike	1987–1993
Hunt, Bernard J.	1965–1966
Hunt, Geoffrey	1964–1965
Hunt, Guy	1973–1973
Huot, Jules	1935–1940
Huston, John	1990–2003
Hutchinson, Denis	1960–1962
Hutchison Jr., Jock	1941–1941
Hutchison, Jock	1935–1959
Hutchison, Ralph	1946–1946
Hyndman III, William	1956–1972
Ilonen, Mikko	2001–2001
Immelman, Trevor	1999–2007
Ingram III, Cecil W.	1980–1980
Inman Jr., Walker	1956–1956
Inman, Joe	1970–1981
Inman, John S.	1985–1994
Irwin, Hale	1971–1996
Isaacs, Jack	1950–1954
Ishii, David	1990–1990
Ishii, Tomoo	1964–1966
Iverson, Don	1974–1976
Izawa, Toshi	2001–2004
Jacklin, Tony	1967–1975
Jackson, James G.	1953–1957
Jackson, Tim	1995–2002
Jacobs, Tommy	1952–1968
Jacobsen, Peter	1981–1995
Jacobson, Fredrik	2004–2005
Jacobson, Gary	1978–1978
Jacobus, George	1934–1934
Jaeckel, Barry	1979–1979
Jaidee, Thongchai	2006–2006
James, Lee	1995–1995
James, Mark	1980–1980
Jamieson, Jim	1972–1974
January, Don	1959–1980
Janzen, Lee	1992–2003
Jenkins, Tom	1976–1976
Jimenez, Miguel Angel	1995–2007
Jobe, Brandt	1999–2006
Johansson, Per-Ulrik	1997–1999
Johnson, Howie	1970–1971
Johnson, Terl	1957–1957
Johnson, Zach	2005–2007
Johnston, Bill	1957–1964
Johnston, Ralph	1974–1976
Johnstone, Tony	1993–1993
Jones Jr., Robert T.	1934–1948
Jones, Grier	1970–1973
Jones, Steve	1988–2001
Kaiser, Bill	1936–1936
Kammer, A. Fred	1948–1948
Kaneko, Yoshinori	1997–1997
Karl, Richie	1975–1975
Karlsson, Robert	2007–2007
Katayama, Shingo	2001–2007
Kay Jr., Jack	1986–1986
Kay, Andy	1935–1935
Kay, Bob	1957–1957
Kaye, Jonathan	2001–2005
Keiser, Herman	1942–1974
Kelly, Jerry	2002–2007
Kelly, John	2007–2007
Kendall, Skip	2000–2000
Kennedy, Les	1950–1950
Kerr, Bill	1961–1961
Kerrigan, George	1934–1934
Kerrigan, Tom	1934–1937
Killian, Michael P.	1973–1973
Kim, Sung Yoon	2000–2000
Kinder, John	1934–1934
King, Rufus	1950–1950
Kirkwood Jr., Joe	1949–1952
Kirkwood, Joe	1936–1948
Kite, Chris	1987–1987
Kite, Tom	1971–2002
Klein, Willie	1935–1935
Knight, Dick	1960–1960
Knowles Jr., Robert W.	1951–1952
Knox, Kenny	1986–1992
Knudson, George	1965–1973
Koch, Gary	1974–1989
Kocsis, Charles R.	1937–1961
Kono, Takaaki	1969–1973
Kovach, Steve	1942–1947
Kozak, Walter	1935–1935
Kratzert, Billy	1974–1986
Kribel, Joel	1998–1998
Kroll, Ted	1951–1962
Krueger, Alvin	1936–1936
Kuchar, Matt	1998–2002

Kuehne, Hank	1999–1999
Kuehne, Trip	1995–1995
Kunes, Gene	1934–1948
Kunkle Jr., Charles	1956–1956
Kuntz, Robert	1954–1954
Lacey, Charles	1934–1934
Laffoon, Ky	1934–1948
Lancaster, Neal	1995–1996
Landrum, Ralph L.	1978–1984
Lane, Barry	1994–1994
Langer, Bernhard	1982–2007
Langham, Franklin	2001–2001
Larrazabal, Alejandro	2003–2003
Lawrie, Paul	2000–2004
Leaney, Stephen	2004–2004
Ledesma Jr., Jorge C.	1963–1963
Legrange, Cobie	1965–1966
Lehman, Tom	1993–2006
Lema, Tony	1963–1966
Lenczyk, Ted	1955–1955
Leonard, Justin	1993–2006
Leonard, Stan	1952–1965
Levet, Thomas	2003–2006
Levi, Wayne	1980–1991
Lewis III, Charles F.	1961–1961
Lewis Jr., Jack Weston	1967–1969
Lewis Jr., Robert C.	1981–1988
Lewis, J. L.	2004–2004
Liang-Huan, Lu	1969–1975
Lickliter, Frank	1999–2002
Lietzke, Bruce	1977–1995
Lind, Charles	1947–1947
Lindley, Brian R.	1982–1982
Lindsey, Pat	1984–1984
List, Luke	2005–2005
Lister, John M.	1971–1977
Little Jr., Lawson	1935–1957
Littler, Gene	1954–1980
Locke, Bobby	1947–1952
Loeffler, Bill	1988–1988
Lohr, Bob	1989–1989
Lonard, Peter	2003–2006
Lott, Lyn	1977–1983
Lotz, Dick	1970–1972
Love III, Davis	1988–2007
Love Jr., Davis	1955–1964
Lowery, Steve	1995–2003
Lunn, Bob	1969–1973
Luther, Ted	1936–1936
Lye, Mark	1984–1990
Lyle, Sandy	1980–2007
MacDonald, Bob	1935–1935
MacDonald, Joe	1947–1947
MacFarlane, Willie	1934–1938
Magee, Andrew	1989–1999
Magee, Jerry	1957–1957
Maggert, Jeff	1993–2005
Mahaffey, John	1974–1990
Mahan, Hunter	2003–2003
Mallory, Leo	1938–1938
Maltbie, Roger	1976–1988
Manero, Tony	1934–1961
Mangrum, Lloyd	1940–1962
Mangrum, Ray	1935–1941
Marr, Dave	1960–1970
Marsh, Graham	1974–1980
Marsh, Kevin	2006–2006
Martell, Henry	1959–1959
Marucci Jr., George	1996–1996
Marusic, Milon	1953–1953
Maruyama, Shigeki	1998–2006
Mason, James T.	1977–1977
Massengale, Don	1967–1973
Massengale, Rik	1969–1978
Matteson, Troy	2007–2007
Mattiace, Len	1988–2004
Mawhinney, Bill	1951–1951
Maxwell, Billy	1952–1966
May, Bob	2001–2001
Mayer, Dick	1951–1967
Mayfair, Billy	1988–2007
Mayfield, Shelley	1955–1957
Mayo, Paul M.	1988–1988
McBee, Rives	1967–1967
McCallister, Blaine	1989–1994
McCallister, Bob	1966–1966
McCarron, Scott	1996–2003
McCoy, James	1956–1956
McCullough Jr., W. B.	1941–1941
McCullough, Mike	1978–1979
McCumber, Mark	1979–1996
McDowell, Graeme	2005–2005
McElhinney, Brian	2006–2006
McEvoy, Peter	1978–1980
McGee, Jerry	1972–1980
McGimpsey, Garth M.	1986–1987
McGinley, Paul	2002–2006
McGonagill, Jim	1949–1949
McGovern, Jim	1994–1995
McGowan, Jack	1965–1965
McGowan, Pat	1981–1984
McHale Jr., Jim	1948–1954
McKnight, Tom	1999–1999
McLean, James C.	1972–1972
McLendon, Mac	1969–1979
McLeod, Fred	1934–1959
McManus, Roger T.	1959–1959
McMullin, John	1959–1959
McNickle, Artie	1979–1980
McNulty, Mark	1988–1997
McSpaden, Harold	1934–1949
Mediate, Rocco	1991–2006
Meeks, Eric	1989–1989
Mehlhorn, Bill	1934–1937
Meister Jr., Edward	1955–1957
Melnyk, Steve	1970–1978
Mengert, Al	1952–1959
Menne, Bob	1975–1975
Meshiai, Hajime	1994–1994
Methvin Jr., Marion C.	1962–1962
Metz, Dick	1934–1959
Micheel, Shaun	2004–2007
Mickelson, Phil	1991–2007
Middlecoff, Cary	1946–1971
Miguel, Angel	1959–1963
Miguel, Sebastian	1961–1964
Miller, Allen	1969–1976
Miller, John	1997–1999
Miller, Johnny	1967–1994
Miller, Lindy	1978–1979
Minoza, Frankie	1991–1991
Mitchell, Bayard	1934–1934
Mitchell, Bobby	1971–1973
Mitchell, Jeff	1980–1980
Mize, Larry	1984–2007
Molinari, Edoardo	2006–2006
Montgomerie, Colin	1992–2007
Montgomery, Brian	1987–1988
Monti, Eric	1950–1962
Moody III, William G.	1980–1980
Moody, Orville	1970–1974
Moore Jr., C. Parker	1977–1977
Moore, Frank	1937–1947
Moore, Ryan	2003–2005
Moreland, Gus	1935–1935
Morey, Dale	1954–1966
Morgan, Gil	1977–1994
Morley, Mike	1967–1981
Morris, Johnny	1942–1942
Morse, John	1995–1997
Mosely, Fred	1949–1950
Mudd, Jodie	1982–1992
Munday, Rod	1940–1946
Munger, Jack	1935–1937
Muntz, Rolf	1991–1991
Murakami, Takashi	1976–1977
Murphy Jr., Bob	1966–1987
Myles, Reggie	1952–1952
Nagle, Kel	1960–1968
Nakajima, Tsuneyuki	1978–1995
Nakamura, Pete	1958–1958
Nakamura, Tohru	1980–1980
Nary, Bill	1948–1954
Nelson, Byron	1935–1966
Nelson, Larry	1979–1992
Newcomb Jr., William K.	1963–1963
Newton, Jack	1976–1981
Nichols, Bobby	1963–1976
Nicklaus, Jack	1959–2005
Nicolette, Mike	1983–1984
Nieporte, Tom	1965–1965
Nobilo, Frank	1995–1998
Norman, Greg	1981–2002
Norman, Murray	1956–1957
Norris, Tim	1983–1983
North, Andy	1976–1990
Norville, Richard S.	1962–1962
Oberholser, Arron	2006–2007
O'Connor Jr., Christy	1977–1977
Ogden, Bill	1954–1957
Ogden, Clay	2006–2006
Ogilvie Jr., David	1934–1934
Ogilvie, Joe	2005–2006
Ogilvy, Geoff	2006–2007
Ogle, Brett	1993–1994
O'Grady, Mac	1986–1988
Ogrin, David	1984–1998
O'Hair, Sean	2006–2006
O'Hern, Nick	2005–2007
Olazabal, José Maria	1985–2007
Oliver, Ed	1940–1960
Olson, Doug	1968–1968
O'Meara, Mark	1980–2007
Ono, Koichi	1958–1963
Onsham, Sukree	1970–1971
Oosterhuis, Peter	1971–1984
Oppermann, Steve	1966–1966
Orellana, Enrique	1964–1964
Ouimet, Francis	1941–1941
Owen, Simon	1979–1979
Owens, John C.	1964–1964
Ozaki, Masashi	1972–2000
Ozaki, Naomichi	1990–2000
Paddock Jr., Harold	1950–1951
Paletti, Joe	1934–1934
Palmer, Arnold	1955–2004
Palmer, Johnny	1942–1957
Palmer, Ray	1954–1954
Palmer, Ryan	2005–2005
Pampling, Rod	2005–2007
Parkin, Philip	1984–1984
Parks Jr., Sam	1934–1962
Parnevik, Jesper	1997–2005
Parry, Craig	1990–2005
Pate, Jerry	1975–1982
Pate, Steve	1988–2000
Patton, Christopher L.	1990–1990
Patton, William J.	1954–1966
Paulson, Dennis	2000–2001
Pavin, Corey	1982–2000
Pearce, Eddie	1972–1976
Peck, Michael H.	1979–1979
Peete, Calvin	1980–1987
Pelissier, Albert	1952–1952
Penna, Toney	1938–1951
Peoples, David	1992–1993
Perelli, John	1934–1934
Perez, Pat	2003–2003
Perkins, Phil	1934–1935
Perks, Craig	2002–2004
Pernice Jr., Tom	1990–2007
Perry, Chris	1984–2001
Perry, Kenny	1992–2005
Perry, Sam	1934–1934
Persons, Peter	1986–1986
Petrovic, Tim	2004–2004
Pettersson, Carl	2006–2007
Pfeil, Mark	1974–1981
Phillips, Frank	1958–1962
Picard, Henry	1934–1969
Pierce, Clifton W.	1984–1984
Pinero, Manuel	1978–1978
Pittman, Jerry	1963–1969
Platts, Lionel	1966–1966
Player, Gary	1957–2007
Ploujoux, Philippe	1982–1983
Podolak, Michael E.	1986–1986
Pohl, Dan	1982–1989
Pooley, Don	1981–1991
Pose, Martin	1940–1941
Pott, Johnny	1961–1969
Poulter, Ian	2004–2007
Price, Nick	1984–2005
Price, Phillip	2004–2004
Pride, Dicky	1995–1995
Pruitt, Dillard	1992–1993
Puga, Greg	2001–2001
Purdy, Ted	2005–2006
Purtzer, Tom	1977–1992
Pyman, Iain	1994–1994
Quick, Smiley	1952–1952
Quigley, Brett	2007–2007
Quinney, Jeff	2001–2001
Rafferty, Ronan	1990–1991
Ragan, Dave	1958–1965
Ramsay, Richie	2007–2007
Randolph, Sam W.	1985–1988
Ransom, Henry	1950–1958
Rassett, Joseph E.	1980–1980
Reasor, Mike	1975–1975
Reavie, Chez	2002–2002
Rebmann, Eric	1988–1988
Refram, Dean	1964–1976
Regalado, Victor	1975–1979
Reid, Mike	1981–1990
Renner, Jack	1980–1986
Revolta, Johnny	1934–1962
Richardson, Steven	1992–1992
Riddell, John	1937–1937
Ridley, Fred S.	1976–1978
Riegel, Robert	1936–1936
Riegel, Skee	1947–1957
Riley, Chris	2003–2005
Rinker, Larry	1983–1986
Robbins, Hillman	1955–1958
Roberts, Loren	1991–2003
Rocca, Costantino	1994–1998
Rodgers, Phil	1958–1975
Rodriguez, Juan	1961–1982
Roe, Mark	1996–1996
Rogers, Bill	1978–1986
Rollins, John	2003–2007
Romero, Eduardo	2001–2004
Rosburg, Bob	1948–1972
Rose, Clarence	1997–1997
Rose, Justin	2003–2007
Rossi, Ricardo	1953–1953
Rudolph, Mason	1958–1974
Ruiz, Leopoldo	1962–1965
Rule Jr., Jack	1964–1964
Rummells, David	1989–1990
Runyan, Paul	1934–1960
Ryan, Jack	1941–1942
Sabbatini, Rory	2001–2007
Sala, Miguel J.	1961–1964
Sander, William K.	1977–1977
Sanders, Doug	1957–1973
Sang, Hahn Chang	1973–1973
Santilli, Angelo	1954–1954
Sanudo, Cesar	1966–1973
Sarazen, Gene	1935–1973
Sargent, George	1934–1937
Sauers, Gene	1987–1993
Scherrer, Tom	2001–2001
Schlee, John	1971–1978
Schneiter, George	1946–1956
Schoux, George	1947–1947
Schroeder, John	1974–1983
Schulz, Ted	1990–1993
Schutte, Warren	1993–1993
Schwartz, W. J.	1934–1935
Scott, Adam	2002–2007
Scott, Steve	1997–1997
Scott, Sydney	1962–1962
Segura, Juan	1951–1951
Selby, Jack	1948–1948
Senior, Peter	1990–1990
Serafin, Felix	1937–1947
Shaw, Bob	1973–1973
Shaw, Tom	1971–1971
Shearer, Bob	1976–1983
Sheppard, Charles	1958–1958
Sherry, Gordon	1996–1996
Shields, Bill	1951–1951
Shute, Denny	1934–1962
Siderowf, Richard L.	1967–1978
Sieckmann, Tom	1989–1991
Sigel, R. Jay	1978–1988
Sikes, Dan	1963–1975
Sikes, Richard H.	1962–1970
Sills, Tony	1986–1990
Silverio, Luis F.	1966–1967
Simons, Jim	1971–1983
Simpson, Scott	1981–1998
Simpson, Tim	1985–1991
Sindelar, Joey	1985–1993
Singh, Jeev Milkha	2007–2007
Singh, Vijay	1994–2007
Sjoland, Patrik	1999–1999
Sluman, Jeff	1988–2007
Smith, Al	1948–1949
Smith, Charles B.	1962–1965
Smith, Horton	1934–1963
Smith, MacDonald	1934–1934
Smith, Nathan	2004–2004
Snead, J. C.	1972–1988
Snead, Sam	1937–1983
Snedeker, Brandt	2004–2004
Sneed, Ed	1974–1983
Somerville, C. Ross	1934–1938
Sonnier, Randy	1985–1986
Sota, Ramon	1964–1972
Souchak, Frank	1954–1954
Souchak, Mike	1955–1966
Souza, Stan K. M.	1977–1977
Spears, Herschel	1949–1950
Spears, Richard A.	1971–1971
Spray, J. Steve	1961–1969
Springer, Mike	1995–1995
Stadler, Craig	1974–2007
Stahl, Walter	1964–1964
Standly, Mike	1993–1994
Stankowski, Paul	1996–1998
Stanton, Bob	1967–1967
Stenson, Henrik	2006–2007
Stevens, C.G.	1934–1934
Stewart Jr., Earl	1952–1955
Stewart, Payne	1983–1999
Still, Ken	1967–1972
Stockton, Dave	1969–1981
Stonehouse, R. S.	1934–1935
Storm, Graeme	2000–2000
Strafaci, Frank	1938–1950
Stranahan, Frank	1946–1959
Strange, Curtis	1975–1996
Strawn, David	1974–1974
Streck, Ron	1979–1982
Stricker, Steve	1996–2007
Stuart, James P.	1991–1992
Sugimoto, Hideyo	1967–1968
Sullivan, Mike	1981–1995
Sutherland, Kevin	2002–2003
Sutton, Hal	1980–2001
Suzuki, Norio	1981–1981
Sweeny Jr., Robert	1936–1961
Sweetser, Jess	1934–1955
Szwedko, Andrew	1941–1941
Tailer, Tommy	1938–1940
Taniguchi, Toru	2002–2003
Tanihara, Hideto	2007–2007
Tataurangi, Phil	2003–2003
Taylor Jr., Frank M.	1957–1961
Taylor, James W.	1990–1990
Taylor, Vaughn	2006–2007
Tennyson, Brian	1991–1991
Tentis, David M.	1984–1984
Tewell, Doug	1980–1989
Thomas, David C.	1959–1967
Thomas, Jeffrey	1994–1994
Thompson, Alvie	1963–1963
Thompson, Joe	1939–1939
Thompson, Leonard	1974–1990
Thompson, Martin S.	1983–1983
Thomson, Jimmy	1935–1946
Thomson, Peter	1953–1969
Thorpe, Jim	1982–1987
Tiso, Pat	1935–1935
Toda, Torchy	1936–1936
Todd, Harry	1947–1953
Tolles, Tommy	1997–1998
Tolley, David T.	1983–1983
Toms, David	1998–2007
Torrance, Sam	1985–1997
Torza, Felice	1948–1954
Toski, Bob	1951–1957
Townsend, Peter M.	1969–1969
Trahan, D. J.	2001–2001
Travieso, Raul	1968–1969
Trevino, Lee	1968–1991
Triplett, Kirk	1996–2005
Trombley, Bill	1953–1953
Tryba, Ted	1996–2000
Turner, Ted	1936–1936
Turnesa, Jim	1946–1962
Turnesa, Joe	1934–1936
Turnesa, Mike	1934–1949
Turnesa, William P.	1934–1940
Tuten Jr., William H.	1984–1984
Tutwiler, Ed	1965–1968
Tway, Bob	1981–2004
Twiggs, Greg	1989–1989
Twitty, Howard	1980–1994
Updegraff, Edgar R.	1962–1970
Urzetta, Sam	1951–1957
Van de Velde, Jean	2000–2000
Van Donck, Flory	1958–1958
Van Pelt, Bo	2005–2005
Veech, Tom	1951–1951
Venturi, Ken	1954–1969
Verplank, Scott	1985–2007
Verwey, Bob	1967–1967
Vickers, James W.	1966–1966
Villegas, Camilo	2007–2007
Vincent, Jimmy	1934–1934
Vines, Ellsworth	1947–1949
Voges, Mitchell C.	1992–1992
Von Elm, George	1951–1951
Von Nida, Norman	1950–1962
Von Tacky Jr., Richard L.	1981–1981
Vossler, Ernie	1956–1960
Wadkins, Bobby	1981–1988
Wadkins, Lanny	1970–1995
Wadsworth, Fred	1987–1987
Waite, Grant	1994–2001
Waldorf, Duffy	1993–2001
Walker, Cyril	1934–1934
Wall Jr., Art	1956–1988
Walsh, Frank	1934–1941
Waltman, Retief	1959–1964
Walzel, Bobby	1981–1981
Ward Jr., E. Harvie	1948–1966
Ward, John	1951–1951
Ward, Marvin	1938–1957
Watabu, Casey	2007–2007
Watrous, Al	1934–1946
Watson, Craig	1998–1998
Watson, Denis	1985–1987
Watson, Tom	1970–2007
Watts, Brian	1999–2000
Weaver, Bert	1965–1965
Weaver, DeWitt	1972–1973
Webb, Gene	1950–1950
Weetman, Harry	1957–1960
Wehrle, Wilford	1940–1940
Weibring, D. A.	1980–1997
Weir, Mike	2000–2007
Weiskopf, Tom	1968–1984
Weitzel, John	1955–1955
Weslock, Nick	1958–1965
West III, Martin	1972–1980
Westland, Jack	1935–1959
Westwood, Lee	1997–2007
Wetterich, Brett	2007–2007
Wettlaufer, H. Ward	1959–1961
White, Buck	1946–1950
White, Orville	1935–1936
Whitt, Don	1958–1958
Wiebe, Mark	1986–1989
Wiechers, Jim	1976–1976
Wilcox, Terry	1970–1971
Wild Jr., Claude C.	1961–1961
Wilkes, Brian	1962–1962
Wilkes, Trevor	1957–1957
Will, George	1966–1966
Williams Jr., Henry	1950–1951
Williams, Harold	1951–1951
Willits, Robert W.	1947–1947
Wilson, C. T.	1934–1934
Wilson, Dean	2007–2007
Wilson, Stuart	2005–2005
Wininger, Bo	1953–1966
Wittenberg, Casey	2004–2005
Wollmann, Chris	1996–1996
Wolstenholme, Gary	1992–2004
Womack, Dave	2007–2007
Wood, Craig	1934–1961
Wood, Willie	1982–1999
Woods, Tiger	1995–2007
Woosnam, Ian	1988–2006
Worsham, Lew	1947–1962
Wrenn, Robert	1988–1988
Wright, Jimmy	1970–1970
Wynn, Bob	1977–1978
Wysong, H. Dudley	1960–1967
Yamamoto, Guy	1995–1995
Yancey, Bert	1967–1975
Yang, Yong-Eun	2007–2007
Yates III, P. Daniel	1989–1993
Yates, Charles	1934–1947
Yost, Richard L.	1957–1957
Zahringer, George	2003–2003
Zarhardt, Joe	1942–1942
Zarley, Kermit	1968–1974
Zender, Robert	1970–1970
Zerman, Manny	1991–1992
Zhang, Lian-Wei	2004–2004
Ziegler, Larry	1970–1977
Zimmerman, Al	1946–1946
Zoeller, Fuzzy	1979–2007
Zokol, Richard	1993–1993

Masters Club Dinner

— III —

Front row (left to right): Arnold Palmer, Doug Ford, Phil Mickelson, Ben Crenshaw, Chairman Billy Payne, Jack Nicklaus, Billy Casper. *Second row:* Tiger Woods, Mike Weir, Vijay Singh, Gary Player, Fred Couples, Bob Goalby, Gay Brewer, Sandy Lyle, Seve Ballesteros, Tommy Aaron, Charles Coody, Nick Faldo. *Third row:* Larry Mize, Mark O'Meara, Craig Stadler, Ian Woosnam, Bernhard Langer, José Maria Olazabal, Tom Watson, Raymond Floyd, Fuzzy Zoeller.

Amateur Dinner

Left to right: John Kelly, Dave Womack, Chairman Billy Payne, Julien Guerrier, Richie Ramsay, Casey Watabu.

Committee Chairmen

Front row (left to right): H. Ray Finney, Edwin L. Douglass Jr., Leroy H. Simkins Jr., Phil S. Harison, Chairman William P. Payne, Joe T. Ford, Fred S. Ridley, James E. Johnson Jr., Charles H. Morris.
Back row: Robert H. Chapman III, Ogden M. Phipps, H. Lawrence Parker, Craig Heatley, J. Haley Roberts Jr., Thomas M. Blanchard Jr., Frank Troutman Jr., W. Lipscomb Davis Jr., John L. Murray Jr.
Not pictured: John H. Dobbs, Eugene M. Howerdd Jr., Hugh L. McColl Jr., George R. Wislar.

Rules Committee

Front row (left to right): Gene Howerdd, John Reynolds, Rob Chapman, Michael Bonallack, Jim Reinhart, Danny Yates, Fred Ridley, Pierre Bechmann, Ian Webb, Walter Driver, Gordon Jeffrey, Geoffrey Yang. *Second row:* Dow Finsterwald, Missy Crisp, Rick Burton, Michael Lunt, Irv Fish, Jim Hyler, Pat McKinney, Loren Singletary, Jim Bunch, Christie Austin, Theo Manyama, Stephen Cox, David Pepper, Andrew Langford-Jones, Jack McDonald, Fred Nelson. *Third row:* John Mutch, M. G. Orender, Charles Lanzetta, David Fay, Mickey Bradley, Sue Ewart, Tommy O'Toole, Jay Rains, Jim Vernon, John Kim, Jim Remy, Ken Lindsay, Andy Yamanaka, Ben Nelson, Martin Kippax, Michael Brown, David Williams, David Parkin. *Fourth row:* Mark Dusbabek, Ed Hoard, Mike Davis, Glen Nager, Ian Pattinson, Peter Dawson, Andy McFee, Kerry Haigh, Steve Smyers, Allen Wronowski, Brian Whitcomb, David Young, David Price, Jim Deaton, John Paramor, Mark Russell, Lew Blakey, Bill Lewis, Mark Wilson, Brad Gregory, Mike Shea. *Not pictured:* Roger Warren.

Golf Writers Association of America

Front row (left to right): Hank Gola, Ed Sherman, Marino Parascenzo, Mike Kern, Dick Mudry, George Sweda, David Mackintosh, Mike Buteau, George Willis, Lew Hege, Joe Logan, Dave Perkins, Mark Herrmann, Jim McCabe, Art Spander, Bud Thompson. *Second row:* Loren Rubenstein, Joel Walker, Mike Dudurich, Gerry Dulac, Pat Larkey, John Davis, Larry Dorman, Cameron Cole, Tim Campbell, Garry Smits, Tod Leonard, Bob Buttitta, Steve Di Meglio, David Barrett, Sal Johnson, Kaye Kessler. *Third row:* Paul Himmelsbach, Judy Himmelsbach, Bev Norwood, Dave Hackenberg, Vartan Kupelian, Bruce Vittner, [Unidentified], Eddie Pelz, Tommy Braswell, Bruce Berlet, Sam Weinman, Tim Cronin, Reid Hanley, Ann Liguori, Elisa Gaudet, Furman Bisher. *Fourth row:* Greg Johnson, [Unidentified], Helen Ross, John Edwards, Scott Gutterman, Lauren Deason, Reiko Takekawa, Sadao Iwata, Art Stricklin, Rick Adams, Jack Berry, Bob Stevens, Dove Jones. *Fifth row:* Gary D'Amato, Terry Moore, Alex Miceli, Marla Ridenour, Roger Graves, T. R. Reinman, Marty Hackel, Bill Fields, Doug Ferguson, Mark Soltau. *Sixth row:* Ron Kaspriske, Max Adler, Randall Mell, Jeff Babineau, Tom Bonk, Grant Hall, Melanie Hauser, Dave Shedloski